# INTEGRITY WITH FIRE

*by*
*Nevers Mumba*

**Vincom, Inc.**
Tulsa, Oklahoma

Unless otherwise indicated, all Scripture quotations are taken from the *King James Version* of the Bible.

*Integrity With Fire*
ISBN 0-927936-55-0
Copyright © 1994 by Nevers Mumba
Victory Ministries, Inc.
P. O. Box 22656
Kitwe, Zambia, AFRICA


Published by VINCOM, Inc.
P. O. Box 702400
Tulsa, OK 74170
918-254-1276

# Dedication

We are a sum total of those things we have learned from others over the years. I am grateful for the team members, friends and workers at Victory Ministries with whom God has surrounded me, men and women of integrity whose information and encouragement helped produce what is in this book.

A special deep gratitude goes out:

To my dear wife Florence and our children Shumoel, Tehillah, Yehoshna, Michael and Natasha for their support, patience, and understanding during my travels outside the home.

To Sue McDermott, my gifted personal secretary, who constantly challenged me to write this book. Her support was invaluable.

To Reinhard Bonnke, for believing in me before I even "knew" myself.

To my father and mother for having brought me up in the fear of the Lord. Their love gave me the confidence I needed to achieve my highest dreams.

# Contents

# Contents

# Foreword

I first met Nevers Mumba in Zambia in 1981 and immediately knew that God had put His mighty hand upon the man. He went to America for his theological studies and has, since then, developed into a man of God with a powerful anointing of the Holy Spirit. His highly successful television ministry, his church work and Gospel crusades reach throughout Zambia and extend across various corners of the world. His ministry has established his excellent reputation.

The book, *Integrity With Fire*, gives us insight into the heart of this anointed servant of the Lord as well as into the secret of his own life's ministry. It is refreshing and inspiring, and I recommend it very much.

*Reinhard Bonnke*

# Preface

We are not yet serious about revival until we face the issue of integrity within the Church, and more precisely, within the Charismatic leadership. A Third World preacher is faced with numerous setbacks in ministry. A distorted self-image, a major lack of finances, and other such factors have literally driven some of the most anointed preachers in the "so-called" Third World countries to compromise their integrity. Exaggeration, Charismatic lies, competition, Charismatic witchcraft, financial mismanagement, and other such vices, have contaminated the quality of ministry. In doing so, they block the stream of spiritual breakthroughs our generation will ever live to experience.

The Third World is about to take the stage for end-time Christian leadership. It has been kept aside for a purpose. It is God's reserve tank to be unleashed against one of the most aggressive and deplorable generations the world has ever known. The Third World Church is pregnant with God's last baby — revival. The missing link in this revival is the subject of this book. It is integrity and character. God's search is not for power preachers but for men of integrity, those who will be held accountable for their words. Nevers Mumba highlights integrity as a major foundation stone of any lasting revival. Without it, revival turns into a wildfire that consumes the innocent!

# Introduction

## Winning a Nation for God
## Through Integrity

Is it possible to walk in integrity and be filled with God's fire and power? The answer is yes. A new breed of leaders is impacting nations today. These leaders are fiery and full of integrity. Preaching alone does not change a nation. Preaching with integrity does.

This book deals with the character necessary to influence a generation. Fire is of God and fundamental to ministry. Fire without integrity becomes a wildfire: pointless and aimless. Integrity with fire is what we need to impact our generation. Jeremiah was such a man. He was a man of integrity because he obeyed God as a prophet — an impossible task in his generation. In spite of his perils, he stood and kept his charge: **...but his word was in mine heart as burning fire shut up in my bones...** (Jeremiah 20:9) was his attitude.

One leading South African pastor said to me recently, "Zambian preachers are great communicators of the Gospel." The statement provoked me to think. Why, then, if we are great Gospel communicators are we having an extremely limited effect on our nation? Some of the best preachers I've ever heard are Zambians. They are anointed and move in the miraculous. However, I have come to realize that God is not looking for ministers only but for ministers with integrity. We cannot force a nation to come to God through our preaching alone. We must move the nation back to God through our lifestyles of integrity. Our generation needs ministers of exceptional integrity. Without it, our efforts and witness are hollow.

What does the word *integrity* mean and how do we make sure we are walking in it? The *Oxford English Dictionary* defines integrity as "wholeness, an unimpaired moral state, freedom from moral corruption, innocence, uprightness, fair dealing, honesty and sincerity." These words are as rare as gold in most of our churches. The anointing does not define the quality of the preacher but character does. Character is integrity on display.

Ask yourself, for example, am I honest in my reports and testimonies? Do I judge myself soberly? Do I tell the TRUTH about others? If you consistently do these things, then you are walking in integrity. Qualities such as these are absolutely important when it comes to our integrity. Our generation's preachers must start living transparently. They must live as if their lives are on display — because they are.

One of the reasons a number of preachers lack integrity is the present competition going on in the Church. To begin to cover this ground, start with a frank evaluation of yourself by answering the following questions. It will show you what I mean. Are you trying to present a different image to people from who you really are? Are you in the business of impressing people?

If you are, you disqualify yourself from the race of world changers. The Bible condemns selfish ambitions and warns us against conceit and high-mindedness. It tells us why they are a trick of the devil who used similar tricks on Jesus in Matthew 4:3. He said, **If thou be the Son of God...** The devil wanted Jesus to perform miraculous feats to prove He was the Son of God. The irony of it is, Jesus knew He was the Son of God so He had nothing to prove to the devil at all.

Look at it this way. If your name is Gabriel Nkandu, that is who you are, whether I agree with you or not. If you are a man of God, you are a man of God. You don't have to prove it by telling a "few lies" on the person you apparently raised from the dead. Preachers need to have a new identity — one of INTEGRITY — to be trusted men of their word.

A couple of years ago a new idea to promote ministry came into the Christian world, especially in Zambia. It turned out to be a false one, though. Some preachers believed that if you traveled overseas, your value increased as a man of God. It quickly became the goal of many. Tickets were borrowed from travel agents to fulfill this new goal and debts were accumulated to follow this foolish notion. The lesson was harsh. Those who tried it found that a trip to America does not make you any more of a man of God than a trip to any other destination within the country. Those who tried this tactic learned how ministry value does not depend on the car you drive, the house you own, the trips you make or the clothes you wear. It depends solely on your standing with God and the state of your HEART toward Him. The two alone decide your worth and authority to influence a nation. Both make up the Integrity Ingredient.

The Integrity Ingredient, then, becomes our authority for taking over a nation. Without it, our labors are vain. The world does not want to hear about God, it wants to see and taste God, to experience His full power. When we speak as ministers, the nations will hear us when they cannot find sin in us. Yes, they will criticize us, accuse us falsely, but in the end they will be forced to say to themselves, he is a man of God. Paul says to Titus, **In all things shewing thyself a pattern of good works: in doctrine shewing uncorruption, gravity, sincerity, sound speech, that cannot be condemned; that he that is of the contrary part may be ashamed, having no evil thing to say of you** (Titus 2:7,8). The major key in possessing our generation is not sermons but demonstration of the life and power of God.

# 1

# Integrity Gives Fire Power

With numerous moral problems surrounding the present-day Charismatic Movement, I would like to affirm to you that you can be full of God's fire in your bones and walk in integrity also. The consensus in the Christian community has been that Charismatics are shallow and morally unstable. I firmly reject this notion and would like to say that receiving the baptism of the Holy Spirit does not exclude you from a purposeful walk of integrity, which should be the quest of every believer — Pentecostal, Charismatic, Baptist or Presbyterian. Lack of integrity is not a denominational problem, it is a problem of personal sin. In this book I will deal with why Charismatics seem morally weak, by unveiling the wisdom of God.

> **Lack of integrity is not a denominational problem, it is a problem of personal sin.**

Scripture says, **The adulteress will hunt for the precious life** (Proverbs 6:26). In military terms, the most dangerous enemy is the one most sought after. The Charismatic Movement is one such enemy to darkness. It has brought a new dedication to God, a renewed interest in prayer and fasting, and a greater desire to study scripture than ever before. It is a raging fire that sends us out beyond our religious borders. The enemy camp has not been under as much pressure as it now is, under the Charismatic Movement. Never, in the history of the Church, have we seen so many conversions to Christ since the death of its founding fathers. Reinhard Bonnke, out of whose life I have personally drawn so much growth and fire for evangelism, has seen crowds of up to half a million people in a single service. History is being made in our generation and we know it not. In respect to the enemy camp, I ask you, who would you say is the devil's greatest enemy? The man influencing nations for Jesus Christ in a manner like Brother Bonnke, or a "well-established" religious priest who doesn't give any "trouble" to the devil? Of course, the best answer is the battlefield evangelist. He is the one who gets the greatest attacks. That truth forms the basis of this book.

We are at war. We have an enemy. He is not concerned with private or retired army officers. He is looking for Generals to strike down, a confirmation of the scripture which says, ...**smite the shepherd, and the sheep shall be scattered**... (Zechariah 13:7). Striking the head first is always the devil's strategy.

Let me give you a vivid illustration of my point. When a prominent televangelist came face to face with the enemy's "bullet," a lot of people said, "Well, we always knew that he was a hypocrite. He never meant anything he preached" I totally disagree with this concept and see it in a completely different light. While this minister cannot blame anyone for his actions, I want you to consider the territory he stepped into. It was dangerous enemy territory. He inflicted daily damage on the enemy's strongholds. The man almost covered the whole world with the uncompromised preaching of God's Word. The enemy was hurt by it. Millions of lives were touched by his broadcasts. Lives were saved and healed, children were fed and educated, clinics and hospitals were built and much more. If the devil has any planning abilities at all, it would be obvious to him that a man like this should be at the top of his hit list. And he was.

Of course, the minister could have avoided his downfall by walking in discipline and integrity. It goes without saying that he should have. Nevertheless, he was targeted by Satan for assault. The Charismatic Movement, likewise, is targeted by the enemy. Therefore, the message of self-discipline and integrity needs to be preached to us more than ever before.

The anointing God placed upon our lives to help us discharge our God-given responsibility is potent but it is also fragile. As we become visible, the masses fix their gaze on our conduct and lifestyle. Discipline, a fruit of the Spirit, enables us to pursue His holiness and righteousness in truth.

# 2

# Score With a Vision

The story of Hannah in 1 Samuel underscores the message of this book. She sought for a single achievement — a baby. She saw the baby before it was conceived. Her vision for a baby brought a baby. Her story is worthwhile as it stresses the need for a vision and the determined will and favor of God to achieve it.

When God created man, His ultimate purpose was for man to multiply and have dominion over all of God's creation.

**And God blessed them, and God said unto them, Be fruitful, and multiply, and replenish the earth, and subdue it: and have dominion over the fish of the sea, and over the fowl of the air, and over every living thing that moveth upon the earth.**

**Genesis 1:28**

Dominion was, and still is, God's ultimate purpose for each one of us. Regardless of color, race, or geographical location, we are all born to have dominion, to rule over the affairs of our individual lives. The question, posed in light of this divine command, is "Why do some Christians excel and others don't?"

For the most part, those who fail to make it spiritually, socially and physically lack foresight. They cannot see where they are going. They lack vision. Being without a vision is the greatest tragedy in any life. Proverbs 29:18 puts it this way, **Where there is no vision, the people perish.** In other words, people without a vision cease to live. Why is vision so important? It gives purpose to your race. If you can see the finish line, you hold the courage to keep running the course you are destined to run in life. Regardless of the opposition, when you can see where you are going, you have the hope of getting there, and no man can stop you. Hannah's story demonstrates this well.

Hannah's vision was to have a baby. She saw the baby in her spirit. When she went to the temple, her one and only need filled her soul. Hannah **Singleness of vision is** knew her priority and was not **a sure sign of victory.** moved from it. She desired, not shoes, but a baby; not fame, but a baby. Her vision was clear and single. Singleness of vision is a sure sign of victory. I learned this reality in school.

My life in Bible college turned out to be routine. Each morning starting at 5:00 a.m., I was in the prayer chapel. One day as I was racing around in the prayer room in violent prayer for my country, I saw myself on the running track, tired but full of hope because I could see the finish line. Sweat covered my body, and I found myself hearing others running behind me. Being aware of them brought untold energy into my body. I ran until I cut across the red ribbon to victory. Then I heard a voice speak into my spirit. "Son, I am sending you back to your country to demonstrate My power and to disciple your nation." That moment was the beginning of beginnings for me. I returned home with purpose. Although I was unsure of how and where to begin, that vision had filled me with supernatural confidence.

That commission from the Lord is as fresh today as it was then. Once a television interviewer asked me, "How did you manage to get to that place **Without a goal you** of spiritual prominence?" My **will never score.** answer was, "I understood my purpose in life in that Bible college prayer room." I knew God had given me a mandate to disciple my nation. His commission has sustained me and kept my focus single. I have tried to do nothing else since then except what God told me in that prayer room. I have scored because I had a goal. The opposite is also true:

without a goal you will never score. Fortunately, Hannah understood this and brought the Prophet Samuel into the world.

The challenge to many Third World Christian leaders is to lay hold of a single-focused vision. Africa has some of the most anointed preachers of our time. Yet, fire without direction becomes wildfire, and wildfire is destructive to everyone around. Third World leadership needs to have a definite direction to be effective in our generation.

How do you get a vision, and how do you know you are following your God-ordained vision? The Apostle Paul voiced similar concerns when he said,

> **I therefore so run, not as uncertainly; so fight I, not as one that beateth the air.**
> **1 Corinthains 9:26**

His concern was that of purpose for his life. You see, the very fact that you are born is enough evidence that God has a specific purpose for your life. All you need then is a vision. Without a vision, your life becomes purposeless. How do you get a vision? You get it from God Who has His original plan for you.

Do you know why God showed me my purpose in that prayer room in Dallas? Because I went to Him in persistent prayer asking Him to open up His treasure box for my life. When you show sufficient interest in knowing your personal vision, God will meet you at your point of need. He has a plan which is the road map for your life. It is to be approached in consistent prayer to God for a revelation of it. Hannah understood this. She had a desperate need for a baby. By knowing God had her answer, she became pregnant with the baby before she actually conceived.

Here is the secret. Do you want to get your road map from God? Get pregnant with a fulfilled life. Be like Hannah. She was so consumed with her need that food lost its taste. Her body turned into one intense desire for God to intervene. She stood in faith with a specific goal in mind — the baby. With her faith and her goal, she scored.

Naturally, understanding was at work too. The Priest Eli, for example, took her for a drunk because of her "unbecoming" behavior. Her yearning, coupled with fasting, made her appear intoxicated. You see, she suppressed the demands of the flesh by going on a fast to intensify her prayer.

I want to put in a word of caution here on present-day fasting. Most of it is prompted by fear over having not fasted in a long time. The object of such a fast is thus carnal and selfishly motivated. It will not yield the results outlined in Isaiah 58. A purposeless fast only **Let's pray through.** achieves some measure of weight loss. A fast that is, on the other hand, the result of a consuming burden literally steals your appetite for food. Our generation, for the most part, is incapable of handling such burdens long enough or the right way. It is a "fast food" generation. One phrase that came out of the old Pentecostal days says, "Let's pray through." This meant you didn't quit until you had broken through. It may sound old-fashioned, but it is still the only way to receive from God.

When your need consumes you, steals your appetite and drives you to the altar to conceive the object of your prayer, then comes the breakthrough. Given the time it needs to mature in your spirit, it will bring forth the petition requested of God. Hannah did not physically receive her baby at the altar, but spiritually she did. The seed was planted during prayer when something broke the burden in her heart. At this point, she knew it was as good as done. She could have gone to buy diapers. How did she know? She concentrated on her petition and pressed in the Spirit to the very heart and soul of God. A single focus brought her reward.

When I was in secondary school, we learned about reflection and light. I will never forget the experiment my science teacher conducted years ago. He used a magnifying glass to arrest the rays of the sun and filtered them through the glass. As long as the light rays were all over the paper, there was no specific effect, but when the beam was concentrated into one sharp ray, the paper would burn. His experiment has remained fresh in my mind. I learned that when you concentrate on one thing, you will penetrate every obstacle, and your work shall become visible.

Lack of vision on our part has hindered God from honoring our "universal prayers." Without vision, prayers are ceremonial. Without vision, prayers lack tenacity. Without vision, one can never overcome opposition. A visionless attitude has ruined Third World countries.

Since they don't see the future, everything happens by chance. Life, though, is more than just a one-time event. It is the unfolding of God's road map for your course. You may not arrive at your vision quickly but hope keeps you alive until you do. Single-mindedness needs to come back to the Church for it to achieve its vision for Christ.

The nation of Israel doesn't seem to have this problem. The nation of Israel is different from all other nations of the world because it is a nation of **If you move without** promise. On account of this, it has **a destination, you** a goal and purpose. Both give the **can never arrive.** nation its direction and vision. Like Israel, you need the promises of God to give your life hope and purpose. He will tell you what He has planned for you and give you direction. The question you need to ask yourself today is, "Where am I going?" If your answer is, "Well, I am not too sure right now," then don't move until you have a destination. If you move without a destination, you can never arrive. Until you discover your purpose in life, you have not begun to live; you are only existing. My vision has kept me going on my life's track. So will yours.

God said to me many years ago, "Son, go and disciple your nation." I returned to my home country, Zambia, in 1984 and established Victory Bible Church on His Word. Since then, other churches have been birthed across the nation. I held evangelistic campaigns in stadiums, auditoriums, arenas, and started a Bible college to train young men and women in disciplining a nation. In 1990 we started our weekly nationwide television broadcast which yields tremendous reports of salvation and healing. In the past few years, our country has been transformed from a mere religious nation to one filled with the knowledge of the glory of God.

The born-again experience has penetrated every strata of society, education, art, media, and politics. Zambia's spiritual landscape has changed. For the first time Zambia has produced a born-again president. It has been said that any given government is a mirror of the generation that put it in power. If this is true, then the very fiber of my nation, Zambia, has been affected by the uncompromised preaching of God's Word. Our vision and cry has been single: "Zambia Shall be Saved," and it is being saved. Still, there is much more to be done. James helps me conclude this great thought of vision.

> **But let him ask in faith, nothing wavering. For he that wavereth is like a wave of the sea driven with the wind and tossed. For let not that man think that he shall receive any thing of the Lord. A double-minded man is unstable in all his ways.**
>
> **James 1:6-8**

You need a goal to score.

## Vision: A Yardstick to Purpose

Vision is a means to reaching your purpose. Vision will not mean a thing to you unless you understand your purpose. The best way to understand your purpose is to go to the book of beginnings and see how it all began. The question to answer would be: What was God's ultimate purpose in creating man?

The answer is laid out in Genesis 1:26. God said, **Let us make man in our own image...and let them have dominion over...all...** There it is. God ordained men to have dominion over all of God's handiwork. In simple terms,

God made you to dominate, to rule over, and to be above only and not below. God's ultimate purpose for you is for you to be in charge of things and circumstances affecting you, to dominate and not to be dominated.

Now God is not speaking to a specific race, tribe, color, or even a gender, but to all of His creation regardless of their geographical location. All of us are to have dominion. Some people have taken this to mean they are to have dominion over men, but that is not what God is saying in the book of Genesis. He means to have dominion over all the earth, apart from your fellow man, who is your joint-heir in dominating the earth. Why then have certain races taken advantage of other races? Many factors have brought this about.

First, it begins when one man uses his substance to control others and to dominate them. Second, the lack of understanding of one's purpose makes him vulnerable to abuse by another. Purpose gives you identity and the courage to think for yourself.

Most of the Third World, for example, is dominated by the West chiefly because their purpose has been distorted. Living on handouts, which they mainly do, dissolves your identity. Once your identity is lost, your purpose is lost too. Not having the riches your neighbor has doesn't make you less important than him. You are still a man or woman of purpose, no matter what your life station is. There are two sides to the purpose coin, however, and both involve power. There is the controlling power and the controlled power. The controlling power may be seen in the following example.

A financier says, "If you want help from me, or a favor, bow before me and do what I want." Sound familiar? It should. Those similar words were used by the devil in Matthew. 4:9. The devil, who is called the god of this world, said to Jesus, . . .**all these things will I give thee, if thou wilt fall down and worship me.** In return for support, homage must be paid to wealthy donors. This is why in our

ministry I have refused to be controlled by so-called
                          "powerful donors," especially if
**A man of purpose is**   they demand it. Such ungodly
**a man of authority.**   control is the devil's principle. Here
                          is the positive side. Jesus did not
bow to the devil because He knew His purpose in life. He
was not intimidated, nor impressed, by the riches of the
enemy. He was fixed on the purpose He announced in Luke
4:18,19:

> **The Spirit of the Lord is upon me, because he hath
> anointed me to preach the gospel to the poor; he hath
> sent me to heal the brokenhearted, to preach deliver-
> ance to the captives, and recovering of sight to the
> blind, to set at liberty them that are bruised, to preach
> the acceptable year of the Lord.**

A man of purpose cannot be stopped or intimidated.
A man of purpose is a man of authority.

The other side of the coin is the controlled. Since his
purpose has been dissolved, he moves with a bait in his
mouth. I have found being controlled more hurtful than
anything else. Lack of economic power has cost the Third
World its identity. The West rules through media, education,
art and political philosophies. The Third World has been torn
up by slavery and colonization which took away most of its
dignity.

# 3
# Strategy

The Lord has allowed me to take the Gospel to many parts of the world, and in almost every country I have identified a new breed of Christian leaders who not only have a vision and a purpose, but they have the strategy needed to walk in the vision and to reach their purpose. Understanding the vision alone does not guarantee you success in fulfilling your purpose. You can have the greatest of intentions, but so long as they are not worked out practically, your vision's fulfillment will be a nightmare.

When God gave me the present vision of discipling my nation, He supplied all the necessary requirements for the challenge. He gave me His anointing, His presence, His Word and His grace. What He did not give me was the details on how to disciple my nation. Here is where many people drop out of the race. Misunderstanding the sovereignty of God has kept many believers from achieving their maximum. Yes, God has given me a vision, so what? Such indifference is fatal to their vision. The attitude has caused millions of people to die with fantastic dreams and visions still lodged in their hearts. One friend of mine says, "The graveyards of the world are the richest places on earth." Great ideas lie buried under the earth. The reason: they failed to work out the vision. Strategizing is a most crucial step because this is where God counts on your creativity to carry out His plan. This is the reason why God gave Holy Ghost-filled believers brains in the first place. It may sound ironic, but when I received the baptism of the Holy Ghost, I started to wonder why God bothered giving me brains. I seriously never thought I would need them anymore once I had the Holy Ghost. Thanks to God He never sucked my brains out. If He had, I could never have fulfilled the vision He gave me. Aren't you glad God doesn't answer all your prayers?

Vision allows you to see the path to your life's purpose. However, it is strategy that makes you reach your purpose and thereby achieve your vision. **Strategy is the plan you use to achieve your purpose.** Strategy is the plan you use to achieve your purpose. Dominion is the general purpose for mankind, but strategy is the individual's application of godly wisdom to achieve God's purpose. Vision and purpose are permanent, but strategy is not. It is simply the best plan to achieve your purpose at a given time. It may change from situation to situation. For example, during war, strategies change depending on the nature of the enemy, terrain or the intended purpose of the battle. The same holds true for the purpose of carrying out a vision.

God called me at the age of seventeen while in high school. I knew God's seed in my life was to preach. Nevertheless, it remained my responsibility to narrow my call to the level of practicality needed to do so. I knew I had to have a strategy. Sometime later while sitting outside my classroom during break, I had an encounter with God. At that time, He gave me what I call an open vision. In a moment, I was raptured to another place. God took me into a live crusade service. (Then I had no idea what a crusade was. I was a comfortable youth leader in our local Assembly of God Church.) With my eyes wide open, I saw a sea of black faces looking intently at me as I stood on the platform with a Bible in my hand. There were thousands of them with tears in their eyes and hands lifted toward heaven. While I marveled at this spiritual phenomena, I heard the voice of God in my spirit saying, "Go, son, go and do it."

Immediately, the whole vision disappeared from before me. Up until this time, I had never seen such a crowd gathered for the Gospel. The vision, I understood, was to confirm the call of God on my heart and to show me what was to come. But, how was I to work it out?

Here is where strategy comes in. Yes, you can know your purpose in life, but to practically fulfill it you need strategy. While I was still an elder and youth leader in the Assembly of God Church, I felt a stirring in my spirit, a call to go beyond my normal limits of just being an elder.

In my youth group there was a young man who owned and played an accordion. I sat with him one day and asked if he could join me in some evangelistic activities, and he consented. The following weekend, we launched our first evangelistic thrust. We went to an overcrowded open market, chose a shady tree, and began the service. Behind the tree was a man selling lucky charms, heads of birds and weird dead creatures. The smell coming from that enterprise was sickening; nevertheless, it was the best spot for our purposes because it was next to a small path used by hundreds of people. So, we stuck it out.

My friend pulled out his accordion and began playing. Back then this was a totally new approach to evangelism. We had, up till this time, only brought evangelists into our local churches and invited some friends to attend their services. Now we went into streets where the action was. Soon, a crowd started to gather. Before long, over a hundred enthusiasts had gathered around my song leader. Meanwhile, I was hiding behind the tree with the Bible tucked away in my sweater. I didn't want anyone to be scared away by it, so I just lingered in the background until the most opportune time. At just the right time, I stepped forward, opened the Bible to John 3:16 and preached my first evangelistic sermon. There were no homiletics, just a clear hell or heaven message. As I delivered a frank take-it-or-leave-it type of sermon, to my amazement, more than fifty people responded to the call of salvation. Then I moved into the healing session. A line of more than twenty was formed! I prayed fervently for each one. So much happened under that tree, I often fondly look back and thank God for it. By the time I was finished praying for the sick from the first crowd, a new crowd had gathered, and I had to start all over again. I continued until it was too dark for me to read the Bible. Thus began our present ministry. My strategy worked and God's vision for my life was launched.

In the first month, we had hundreds of decisions for Christ and found we did not know what to do with them. We decided to start a mail follow-
**Strategy is key**    up ministry. The vision began
**to success.**        taking shape because I did not sit
                       to wait for the angels of God to
come and work out the details for me. Strategy is key to success. God gives you the vision, but you must strategize to reach it. It is God's way, and the Bible is full of God's strategists.

One such strategist is Joshua. He happened to be one of God's greatest. God, after presenting Himself to Joshua, spelled out the purpose for him. He said, "I have given you Ai, go and possess it." It was a simple command. What is interesting to note is, at that point, He did not give Joshua the details on how to do it, only the word: "Go and possess Ai." Let's look further at how Joshua translated his purpose to strategy.

## Joshua, God's Strategist

Let us follow Joshua's steps into further victory. Remember, the story of Ai comes after two contrasting events: the falling of the walls of Jericho, and the later defeat of Joshua's army because of Achan's sin. God's instructions were brief. Let's look at them:

> And the Lord said unto Joshua, Fear not, neither be thou dismayed: take all the people of war with thee, and arise, go up to Ai; see, I have given into thy hand the king of Ai, and his people, and his city, and his land: And thou shalt do to Ai and her king as thou didst unto Jericho and her king: only the spoil thereof, and the cattle thereof, shall ye take for a prey unto yourselves: lay thee an ambush for the city behind it.
> **Joshua 8:1,2**

The Lord said to Joshua, "I **have** given you the king of Ai, his people, his city and his land." When God speaks, it is final. Man makes it a final practicality in this world though. God planted the vision, man came up with the strategy. God said, "You shall do to Ai as you did to Jericho." If some of our leaders today would hear this instruction from the mouth of God, they would come out of the prayer room shaking with a long holy face for everyone to know they heard from God.

The first thing they would do is to organize an arrangement similar to that of the Jericho wall victory, start marching around Ai in silence, and later on give a victory shout. All of them would have died for doing so, because they had not taken time to come up with the strategy needed for their purpose and circumstances. You might argue that God said it, so what was wrong? While God has said a lot of things, we need to do our part, however, to bring them to pass for our mission and our time.

As you can see from this example, strategy is crucial. Joshua recognized that each challenge was different and needed its own original strategy in **God's will for you is** his mission for God. He had the **to have victory.** Word of God in his hand, but he had to have an appropriate strategy. The same is true for us today. God's will for you is to have victory, but you must agree with God by coming up with a strategy that achieves God's will for your life and its purposes.

Joshua's strategy is a classic one. He didn't say, "Well, gentlemen, God has spoken and He is bound to His Word. Let's walk into Ai and take over the city." He strategized in addition to receiving God's Word. He divided the army into two. One group of five thousand was to lay an ambush on the west side of the city. The other group, under his direct command, would approach the city openly but cautiously. Joshua said when they come against us, we shall flee as it was at first when they overcame us. Joshua 8:15-17 records how the strategy worked. They approached the city as before and the king of Ai rose up to fight against Joshua, but fled and all the men of war in Ai pursued after Joshua leaving a city without guard. Joshua stretched forth his spear and the ambush arose quickly. Entering the city, Joshua and his army took it and set it on fire. When the soldiers of Ai looked back, their city was ablaze. So they abandoned their pursuit of Joshua and started off for the city. By this time the ambush group was coming in for an attack. The people of Ai could not run in any direction because they were sandwiched between Joshua's two battalions.

What a victory! It thrills my soul. Victories for God are strategized. Don't wait for angels to come and strategize for you. God showed me the power of strategy in my early years of ministry. When He spoke to me **Victories for God** in the Bible school prayer room, He **are strategized.** said "Go and disciple your nation." It was up to me to sit and count the cost of fulfilling God's Word in my life. The easiest thing would have been for me to return to my country and start to tell everyone that God has given me the nation to disciple, but it wouldn't have brought the results.

For many years now, I have spent the month of January in seclusion, prayer, and fasting to determine the best way to fulfill God's call in my life. My first "major" crusade, after I returned from Bible school in America, had five hundred people in each service. At the time it was a breakthrough. We immediately set up a series of crusades in many surrounding towns. The goal was consistency. A team was put together to travel with me and the vision of discipling my nation was on my heart.

I soon realized, however, that I could not achieve it single-handedly. A Bible school was born with five young men who traveled with me in our crusades. In the mornings I would teach them all I knew and learned in Bible school. They were my hope for a continued ministry. I poured into them every resource, finance, time and all the love I had. In the afternoons they went around inviting people to the crusade while witnessing to them on the streets. Their classroom was wherever the next crusade was or the verandah of my home when we were at base. When they graduated, they became a reliable source of leadership and support for me. All five of them are great Christian leaders on three continents of the world serving the Lord. Since this first mobile class, hundreds of students have been trained in our resident Victory Institute of Biblical Studies and charismatic leadership is being sent into every corner to have a part in discipling the nation. Crusades, Bible school, and church planting were all part of the strategy to disciple a nation, and so fulfill the Lord's vision for me.

In late 1980, while I was in prayer at home, I felt a great impression on my heart. God was speaking to me. I heard Him ask, "Do you want to be known or become popular?" Of course you can guess my answer, "Oh, no Lord — only You should be popular, not man. I would rather decrease so that you could increase." Then God asserted His intention and said, "For the sake of My name, I will make you known." I knew God was speaking to me, but could not see why God would want to make a man popular. Then God said, "If you will seek to please Me and represent Me for the rest of your life, I will lift you up, so that when people see you, they actually see Me in you. When people hear the name Nevers Mumba, they immediately think of My goodness and power; the more they hear and see you, the more they will hear and see Me." I had never seen this before. The responsibility was heavy on me because I realized that if the opposite happened, I could bring shame on the name of the Lord. I knew God was confirming His approval of my strategy.

Recently I attended a funeral. In African culture women are usually inside the houses and the men sit around a fire outside all night long. I decided to join the women to pray with them. While I was sitting there, a five-year-old boy woke up from sleep. His eyes fell on me straight from his sleep, and he exclaimed in a loud voice, "This is Nevers Jesus" I was stunned, but the boy had seen me on television and had made a direct connection between Nevers and Jesus — God's Word was performed. All I talk about is Jesus during our broadcasts. My point is, if you stand for Jesus, they will mistake you for Jesus. It is God's idea that we be transformed and be the expression of His love and mercy. How will God achieve this? Strategy, that's how.

On January 6, 1990, our first television broadcast aired nationally. The message was evangelistic, "What Is Your Name?" It sent ripples of conviction across the nation, bringing in a mighty harvest of souls for the Lord. Our counseling lines jammed until after midnight. We went down in history as the first national ministry to have a television broadcast. The television strategy solidified our efforts to disciple our nation for God. Our radical weekly broadcast made news, and the newspapers covered it. We got free publicity from them. Miracles of healing spread across the nation as a fire would. Our crusade crowds grew from the original five hundred to over twenty thousand in our Lusaka crusades.

The Gospel has power, but we need to learn the art of strategy. Our generation has some of the most powerful preachers but most of them lack the ability to plan, to strategize. Most Third World ministries lack financial support because they lack direction. People want to support someone who has direction and strategy. Preaching without strategy is like building a house without a plan. You may eventually build it but it may take you a century to do it or it will collapse during dedication. Effective, deliberate planning is at the root of every successful ministry. Ask yourself, "What do I want to achieve? How can I achieve it in the shortest time possible?" From here, you plan, then build. Remember, strategy will change depending on the circumstances, but keep your vision clear.

**Preaching without strategy is like building a house without a plan.**

# 4

# The Integrity Concept

Integrity to me means an upright walk, where you can say as Jesus did . . . **for the prince of this world cometh, and hath nothing in me** (John 14:30). The loss of personal purpose makes the quest for integrity without effect. Why should I walk right before God and man when my future looks bleak? Why should I be honorable when everybody else is taking advantage of the other? Can a battle for righteousness prevail over the ongoing trend of unrighteousness and injustice?

One of the major keys to a life of integrity is the reorganization of our priorities. When we make God's priority ours, then we have a reason to walk in integrity. The **When we make God's priority ours, then we have a reason to walk in integrity.** Church world has never had its priorities as mixed up as it does now, and this is the source of the many problems in the Church today. Genesis 3 helps us to understand why. It depicts the darkest hour of humanity when man rebelled against God. From this day on, God established His priority — to reconcile the human race back to Himself. An innocent animal was killed to facilitate reacceptance of the human race. The entire Bible, as a matter fact, is a summary of God's priority of bringing man back into fellowship with Himself. All the sacrifices, all the ceremonies, all the priests, and all the rituals were instituted to fulfill this priority.

God's priority was culminated in the New Testament when God laid down the most expensive of all sacrifices for the human race. He didn't have to do it; but as the Bible says, **For God so loved the world, that he gave his only begotten Son** (John 3:16). God's

**God's priority is the salvation of the human race at any cost.**

priority is the salvation of the human race at any cost. When you make God's priority your priority, then God's hand will constantly be on your life. Then scriptures like,

**No weapon that is formed against thee shall prosper** (Isaiah 54:17) become a reality. There is no price too high to pay when you are fulfilling God's priority. Money, time, even your own physical life, no longer count when it comes to fulfilling God's priority. God demonstrated the seriousness of the matter by allowing Jesus to die on the cross. A believer, church or ministry that makes God's priority their priority will become one of God's favorites.

Someone might say, "Oh, no, God has no favorites." This may be true to a point. However, those who do God's will become God's best friends. The choice is ours. The Bible says, **Draw nigh to God, and he will draw nigh to you** (James 4:8). Let's look at the story of John, the beloved disciple. Why is he known as the beloved disciple if God is no respecter of persons? There must have been something that made his walk with Jesus different from the others, and there was. The difference between him and the rest of the disciples is that he decided to become Jesus' boy. His goal was to please the Lord. When Jesus sat at meal with His disciples, the Bible says, "John's head was in the bosom of Jesus." Whenever any disciple had a question for Jesus, and vice versa, the answer would come through him. He made Jesus Christ his priority and Jesus made John His.

The Church today is endangered by sloppy priorities. In the Western church, gymnasium constructions, laying thicker carpets, improving and trying to maintain abnormal lifestyles have preoccupied the Body of Christ. They have

taken precedence over the many needs of world evange-
lization. Let's face it, American
**God will judge us** churches give to God more than
**by the souls we win** any other nation I know. Yet com-
**to His Kingdom.** pared to what America spends on
itself and its maintenance of the
highly sophisticated Body of Christ, what it gives for the
actual work of evangelism is only a pittance. What they
spend on themselves, in many cases, far outweighs what
is put toward souls. Souls, we all know, are what God's
priority is all about. God will judge us by the souls we win
to His Kingdom, so we must judge others the same way,
"by their fruit." It is the only way to judge; any other way
would be unfair.

Presently the American church has more opportunities
to influence and change the world for Jesus than any other
nation, but its priorities are messed up. The American
government is more serious about influencing the world with
its philosophies, systems and ideologies than the American
church. The government is well prepared to spend any
amount to achieve its aims. On the other hand, the American
church is preoccupied with blowing trumpets over little
amounts given into missions, just to have something to
report on in their next publication or television program.
In the meantime, the priorities of God wait. God will not
wait forever for America to again focus on God's priority,
which is the salvation of the human race. God is getting
ready to turn the tables. He has to because the Bible says,
**My spirit shall not always strive with man...** (Genesis 6:3).
The American church should look at its advantageous position as an opportunity that can be lost if nothing is done
to fulfill God's priority.

What about the so-called "Third World" church? The
challenges are vast but the pity-party should end. God
planted each one of us where we should be. Africa and other
Third World nations face major drawbacks, lack of finances,
social and political instability and eroded self-esteem due
to an oppressive history. These conditions have created two

situations — one negative, the other positive. The negative is the lack of facilities and finances. It has turned the issue of integrity into facilities and finances. It has turned the issue of integrity into a joke. Lies, crookedness, and insensitivity all thrive in the name of survival. The positive side of it has created a tremendous hunger for God's Spirit and intervention. To a Third World believer, it's either God does it or it will not be done. Unfortunate believers are compelled to take such a stance. For the more fortunate, that is not the case.

While in Bible college, I decided to spend some of my holidays in seclusion to pray and fast. I was so hungry for God, I used the entire Christmas break to pray and fast for two weeks. When one of my American friends heard of my plans to remain on campus to pray, he came to challenge my unrealistic decision. He was well-built and fat. He said, "Nevers, I understand you want to spend the next fourteen days without food." I said, "Yes, I want to be with God alone." For me to do this was nothing new. I had been fasting for long periods in my home **Prayer is not for** country. Looking at me, he said, **one group; it is for** "Don't try, you are going to die **every believer.** from starvation!" That shocked me because I thought anyone in Bible school knew the place of prayer and fasting. He said that he didn't fast, yet God always answered his needs. Another friend standing nearby looked at me and said, "Well, I understand why Africans pray so much. If I felt sick, I would go to a doctor. If I were hungry, I would drive to an eating place, and if I were financially broke, I would go to the bank and borrow. As an American, I don't really need to pray as desperately as you do. Africans don't have these privileges." That is one of the biggest lies the devil ever told. Prayer is not for one group; it is for every believer.

## Right and Good

In Deuteronomy 6:18, two vital ingredients in possessing the land are introduced. The Bible says, **And thou shalt do**

**that which is right and good in the sight of the Lord.** The two words are different. When you do both, it shall be well with you. For God to change a nation, He begins with the vessel He's going to use to bring about change. His main concern for you as His vessel is to be well. If it's well with you, then you're able to do exploits for God.

**And that thou mayest go in and possess the good land,** is next. But first you must do that which is right and good in the sight of the Lord. Doing right and good as commanded by God is where we fail today as Charismatics and Pentecostals. We have forgotten about the necessary basics that bring about the will of God. The word "doing right" means the same as when we say live "righteously with God." We are talking about walking in righteousness, good standing and uprightness with God. Then you shall go in and possess the land. In other words, you can't go in and possess the land without living right and doing good in the sight of God. You will try but you will be doing it in your own flesh. Today we are trying to change a nation with our minds and our brains. No wonder nothing much is happening.

The word "right" expounds on the crucial word we need to return to as the Body of Christ. *Integrity. Integrity* is the word we cannot stumble over. It doesn't matter how anointed you are or how many people you've healed or raised from the dead, if you lack integrity, your ministry is short-lived.

**If you lack integrity, your ministry is short-lived.**

It doesn't matter what country you're in either. Whether you're in the West, in the Third World, in the Second World, or the Seventeenth World, you still need integrity to foster the move of God. It's a word that we pronounce but we don't live. We admire it, but we don't take practical steps to possess it.

The word *good,* as in doing good, is as the word *strategy.* So that I could have a better understanding, I looked up the word *integrity* in the *Oxford English Dictionary,* and this is what it says, "It's an unimpaired moral state; freedom from moral corruption; innocence like a baby; uprightness; fair dealing." Many Christians don't deal fairly. You look at deals in the world today and you'll see you get more crooked deals in the Church than you do in the world.

I held a crusade with a friend in another country. Before we held the crusade, I went to survey the place. I shared a room with them in the motel and we talked until 2 A.M. At the end of our discussion, he said something that bothered me a little bit, but it made me laugh at the end. He said, "Brother Nevers, I'm developing a tremendous burden for my country." I asked why. He said, "I want to ask you to do something. Let's pray for God." That didn't make sense to me. He's talking about God. I told him "God doesn't need your prayers." He said, "Brother, after listening to you talk, I feel we need to pray for God, because I know this country. I've been here since I was born. I'm talking about us preachers. Most of us are dealers and crooks. How is God going to change this country with crooks? Let's pray for God." Thank God that He is not mad. Since He knows us, He knows what He's going to do in this land. Uprightness, fair dealing, honesty, and sincerity. Those words describe the meaning of the word *integrity*.

A man named Owen describes this word *integrity* in the dictionary as meaning "mind of God." When you have the mind of God, you're going to walk in integrity, because the mind of God is the mind of integrity. God stands by His Word. God doesn't tell you one thing today and another tomorrow. He doesn't change His mind saying, "Oh, I was wrong; I was just excited the other day." But we do that. "Oh, Brother," says a Christian who vowed rashly, "there was so much joy in the message, I just said I'll give you $5,000, and I don't even have $10." But God backs up His Word. He's got integrity. God means what He says and He wants that to be imparted into us.

Why is it so difficult today to look at some leaders and just admire the way they walk uprightly with sincerity, honesty, and fair dealing? They are getting fewer and fewer. How many of us can say, "Imitate me as I imitate Christ."

People are so afraid to say "imitate me," because they don't imitate Christ themselves.

Let's look at 1 Kings 9:4,5.

> **And if thou wilt walk before me, as David thy father walked, in integrity of heart, and in uprightness, to do according to all that I have commanded thee, and wilt keep my statutes and my judgments: Then I will establish the throne of thy kingdom upon Israel for ever, as I promised to David thy father, saying, There shall not fail thee a man upon the throne of Israel.**

God is speaking. God attaches tremendous significance to integrity, walking uprightly with Him. I know there are people who are serious about being used of God and there are also those who don't care. When I was in Bible college, there were those there who did not even care about the things of God. Not only were they not hungry for God, but they did not even press in for God. They just relaxed and gave up. They didn't look forward to anything except a mundane life. Many people are like that. Not being go-getters, they don't believe God for anything. They just wait for things to happen by chance, which is why nothing has happened to them. You need to be a man of vision who knows where he's going. Do you get on a plane and just let the pilot take you wherever he wants to? No You need to know the route you should take in order to arrive at the place you want to get to.

**God attaches tremendous significance to integrity.**

A friend told me he had designated days of fasting. (He goes to the mountains to fast.) He said, "Last year God told me to introduce another day — a day of thinking. I don't pray, I don't fast, I just sit on the mountaintop and think." I think he's got a point. Some believers could do a lot with thinking. I was brought up in a church where they tried to tell us that if you think too much, you are of the world. That's a lie.

It's important for you to walk in integrity for you to get in and possess the land. If you can walk in integrity, then your own life becomes a message that can change your community. They can insult you, call you names, but at night when they go to bed they shake their heads and say, "He is somebody — there is something different about that gentleman; he walks right with God. He fears God." People should be able to say that about their leader. If you want to be a leader in the things of God, people must look at you and feel challenged. They should see you and say, "There stands a man who knows where he stands."

Why is it so hard for people to walk in integrity today? I believe there are three roots for lack of integrity. The first reason is dejection; the second is deception; the third one is rejection. These are some of the things that make us feel inadequate. They make us feel as if we have to act and be like somebody else and not be ourselves. They cause us to give a false impression so that people can think we are somebody. That is a waste of time. You are what you are.

We are living in a very cosmetic world, especially if you live in America. I met some ladies that just refuse to grow old. They remove all the wrinkles and plastic everything over, and they look as they did 20 years ago. It's a cosmetic society, but you can only do that for a moment. It doesn't matter how young you look. On the inside of you, the years are still passing. The clock inside of you is always correct. You can use all the makeup you can to look as if you are nineteen, but you can never fool yourself. So it's best for you to live the way you should live. Let everybody know who you are. Don't try to be like somebody else. You are you, uniquely made — specially, fearfully and wonderfully made by God.

In Africa we don't have any trouble asking how old somebody is. If you ask a lady how old she is, she tells you. I tried that in Dallas. There was a lady there I used to pray with and I asked her how old she was. You should have seen her face. I didn't know I was offending her. I found out that some people do not want others to know their age. But one day we will know. It may be on your tombstone! You don't need to try to impress the world. That's the reason we fail to walk in integrity.

What is dejection? Dejection is when somebody is unsure about their standing with God. He feels as though he does not qualify. And because he feels an inadequacy in his walk with God, he tries to **Hypocrisy is a waste** make up by acting like he's some-**of time.** body else. He lifts up his hands during worship, but he doesn't feel anything. He knows he's living in sin. I tell students in our Bible college not to waste their time faking it. Hypocrisy is a waste of time. If you feel dejected, unsure of your position with God, take time to work it through with God because you aren't hiding anything from Him.

The Book of John, chapter 13, says Jesus, knowing who He was, where He came from and where He was going, took a towel and a basin of water, went to His disciples and started to wash their feet. Jesus did that because He had no problem with His position with God. He knew He was the Son of God. Nothing could change that. He didn't have to prove to be the Son of God, because He knew He was from God and was going to God. He didn't think it would steal anything from His value to serve others. Today people are afraid to serve others because they feel it will look as if they are servants, or that it will confirm the way they feel about themselves.

When I came over to Dallas for the first time to go to Bible school, I had a scholarship, bless God. They told me to clean toilets. In Africa, not everybody cleans toilets. There are different classes there and we've always believed that cleaning toilets was for the lower class. The lady was so joyous and didn't even blush when she told me, "Nevers, this is what you'll be doing. Move the trash out of the offices, and make sure all the toilets are cleaned."

As I listened to this, I thought I was in the wrong place. I thought, "Why is she telling me to clean toilets? Is it because I'm from Africa? I'll show her that I'm not what she thinks

I am." But after a day or so, the Holy Spirit started to show me something. One thought came to me: *Nevers, if you don't want to clean the toilet, then you should never use it. If you're too high for the toilet, then don't use it. But if you're high enough to use it, you are also high enough to clean it.*

Maybe I received the "toilet anointing," because when I left Bible college, I went on to preach the Word of God. Cleaning toilets didn't steal anything from my anointing. I knew I was somebody in God. In fact, I decided to pray in the Spirit every day as I was there. I'd be scrubbing the toilet and talking in tongues. And somebody would come and have to use the bathroom. I was tested. I would step aside, then go back. You know that's not easy. Somebody just used it and I'd go back to talking in tongues and cleaning. It's the joy of the Lord that keeps you. It didn't steal anything away from me because I knew God loved me. God had given me a vision. Integrity stood firm in the fact that God had called me.

When Satan tempted Jesus, he said, "If you are the Son of God, turn this rock into bread." Jesus did not have to prove to him that He was the Son of God because both He and the devil knew He was the Son of God. Being sure of yourself will keep you from doing things that will compromise your integrity. It's important for you to make sure that you are confident in your walk with God, confident, and without the need to impress anybody.

The second root for lack of integrity is deception. Lying spirits take over in your life. You become a performer. We have become such great Charismatic performers. It's like a circus. We work for the approval of man. We want man to clap us on, and tell us how great we are. Now, that's all part of encouragement in ministry, but there's a danger if you're only looking for the approval of man and not the approval of God. You do things to make people love you; preach messages to make them comfortable, so that you can keep feeling well. If you work for man, you'll be paid and

**A man of integrity does not perform, he ministers.**

rewarded by man. A man of integrity does not perform, he ministers. He does not want to impress anybody because he does not derive fulfillment from the approval of men, but from the approval of God. It doesn't matter how they look at you. If your ways please the Lord, then it is all right. If they don't like me, that's all right.

Through our crusades, we have discovered something. We don't find people without opinion about us. When we asked people if they liked Nevers Mumba, we only got two answers. Either they said, "I like that man, I pray for him, he's something else," or they said, "I hate him, I could choke him to death." Never in between. Whenever the answer's in between, then you're not preaching good enough. Paul never had the in betweens. Either they were lifting him up saying, "Yes, Paul is a great man," or they were stoning him almost to death. Today we don't want that. We want that comfortable life of being appreciated, of not being offensive. If you're not offensive then you're not preaching the Gospel, because the Gospel is offensive.

I like to hear what people think because I'm not moved by what they think. Some people have told me how they pray for me and how much they appreciate us. Last year, we had a big conference and many preachers from various parts of the world came. One of our guests said, "Brother Nevers, I'm so glad I know you because your name works like magic at the airport. When I arrived, I said 'I am going to Victory Ministries.' I asked a female staff member what she thought of your ministry. She said, 'Oh, Pastor Mumba is our Pastor.'" And this guest was able to get things taken care of faster than others. But she could have just as well met somebody who hated me. But that's okay as long as they privately consider me to be somebody in God. Some people never publicly say good about you. Our integrity offends others. Those who are living in sin are generally offended.

Yet, having integrity pays off. One of our guests was taking photographs of his hotel and the police came and escorted him over to the police station. They thought he was a spy and tried to interrogate him. Someone came and told me about what happened. I drove over there and when I arrived, there was the Chief of Police interrogating my guest. The guest was trying to tell him he didn't know he was doing anything wrong by taking pictures. When I got there, the Chief of Police looked at me and said, "Ahh, so you're the Nevers Mumba I've been hearing so much about." Then, he asked me, "What is really happening here?" I said, "This man did not know it was wrong; and as far as I know, it is allowed to take a picture of a hotel." He said, "Oh, Pastor Mumba, were sorry, we didn't know he was your guest. Please take him." And the case ended.

If you establish integrity, you are going to do much for God. Even when they insult you, they know that you still have something to offer. It's not only your message but your life that becomes a strength in bringing glory to God. You cannot be a crook and expect to be used by God. There's a price to pay and it is the price of discipline, a price of walking in integrity.

The last root for lack of integrity is rejection. We have a lot of preachers suffering from rejection. From childhood, they haven't had a good background, and so they see themselves as failures. These are people who like to exaggerate things. When he says, "Oh, we just had a tremendous crusade with thousands of people," what he's really saying is, "Look at me; I am somebody." He gets his value from his activity, not from his position in God. He tries to make himself a man of God because of what he has done or what he has.

Some people use their cars as a means of identity. If you get your value from the car, when the car breaks down, you feel you have lost self-worth and you are no longer a man of God. Learn to walk in integrity, and God will help you. Today, everybody is excited about numbers. You don't have to inflate details of yourself to be somebody. You are already somebody in God. Be honest with yourself. Deal

**Learn to walk in integrity, and God will help you.**

honestly, fairly. If you walk in integrity, people are going to come to you because they see something in your life.

People are really not interested in your success. They would rather know what you can do for them. Know for sure, the more you succeed, the more enemies you will get. Three weeks ago I was being interviewed on television and the interviewer was trying to ask questions to provoke me to say things I should not say. I told her frankly what was happening in our ministry.

You don't have to try to exaggerate things to feel like somebody. Just be faithful and speak the truth. Let God add the icing. We should be committed to influencing our nation and our society. People don't like it when you're making it in life. Don't ever be deceived. Just because you're succeeding in ministry doesn't mean you'll have more friends. The truth is you'll have more enemies than before. Look at Joseph in Genesis 37. There's a revelation in the coat of many colors. He had a lot of enemies. The more he pronounced the blessings of God, the more upset people got with him. This is true, especially with Christians who don't have direction. They get so upset by Christians who do. They get so offended, they call you names.

When we opened our present Bible college, people said, "Well now, I guess Nevers thinks he's a professor." I was just believing God for a few students. There were four young men who followed me wherever I went. So I offered to teach them. For one year I taught them in the back yard of my house. When they graduated, Dr. Wayne Myers came. He got so excited. I was embarrassed that there were only four students. But Brother Myers came and shook my hand and said, "Nevers, you are a man of faith." I said, "Say that again!" I didn't know what all the excitement was about. I had four guests that I taught in the back yard of my house, all that I had learned in Bible college in Dallas. Myers said, "You have really impressed me because you have invested your life in these four young people. Now you are producing leadership." He went back to Dallas and said I was doing a mighty work for God. I didn't tell him to do that.

Mrs. Lindsay, President of Christ for the Nations, later called me from Dallas and said, "Nevers, I hear things are happening over there." I said, "Well, glory to God, we did have a graduation for a 'certain number' of students here. God is doing a wonderful thing here in Zambia." She said, "Nevers, go for it." We found a property and they helped us purchase our first Bible college property. That's how it all began, with faithfulness and, one, two, three or four.

I want you to know that integrity will always see you through. It doesn't matter how small you start, but you must stand through the trials of time. An evangelist once came and stood in my office. He used to **Integrity will always** be a tremendous man of God. He **see you through.** said, "Brother Nevers, I want you to tell me something. You have gone through so much opposition, so many insults and yet you are still about the only evangelist in this country that is getting stronger and stronger. What principle do you use?" He had pastored a church, but he had given up. I answered, "When God calls you to do something, stick with it. Through the fires, no matter the challenge, don't give up. Integrity is going to see you through!"

**And every man that striveth for the mastery is temperate in all things** (1 Cor. 9:25). In other words, what the Bible is saying is this: A man who is going to engage himself in something that he wants to attain must be disciplined and self-controlled. Natural men do so to obtain a corruptible crown — a perishable one. Paul sums it up best when he said, "but we — an incorruptible crown." Meaning, we, believers in Christ Jesus, will receive something of eternal value.

Jesus said, **Without me, ye can do nothing** (John 15:5). When I first read that scripture, I thought, that cannot be true. I knew a lot of unbelievers who did not know God. They cursed Him, didn't give money for the Gospel, and yet they were prospering. How then could Jesus say that without Him a person can do nothing?

As I thought on the passage, God gave me insight into it. When Jesus said, **Without me ye can do nothing,** He spoke of eternal things. What He meant was that without Him, a person could not do anything of eternal value. That is, during the days of their earthly life, they could amass wealth, make a name for themselves, drive the best cars, wear the best clothing, but all those things are vain without Christ. They are perishable, corruptible, like the crown we spoke of earlier. However, the things that really matter are the things that are eternal, what pertains to the Kingdom of God.

Paul's word challenges the children of God by saying, if those people who do not know God discipline themselves to obtain a corruptible crown, how much more should we, His disciples, discipline ourselves to receive the eternal values that God has so wonderfully given us. There is no way you are going to make progress in God until you bring yourself under discipline.

**I therefore, so run not as uncertainly; so fight I, not as one that beateth the air,** says our writer. What he means is, don't run like somebody who does not know where he is going. Plenty of people are running uncertainly, not knowing where they are going. Christians, in this instance, lead the pack. They just run around hoping to hit on something, one day. It is hope called faith, although it is not really faith at all. Clearly, the Bible teaches that faith without works is dead. What Paul is saying, therefore, is whenever you see me, I'm fighting my way in the natural. But, I've got a supernatural goal and my eyes are set to attain it. You, too, must have a goal and be able to see it in order to take the ball in that direction.

The Holy Spirit spoke to my heart, "Son, do you know that the only key to these people **When was the last time you believed something?** receiving their miracles and changing from point A to point B is one word — belief?" I ask you, when was the last time you believed something? Believing is important, it is vital. Believing

releases the hand of God to move and act on your behalf.
You can change your position from being poor to being rich
simply by believing that all the cattle on a thousand hills
belong to God. What you believe is what you are going to
be...so believe. Sometimes we think we believe, but we
don't really. What we actually do is sympathize instead.
When it comes to the Gospel, we merely sympathize with
it. We don't act on it, which is what it takes for it to become
a living reality of our faith. You see, when you believe, you
become like what you believe eventually, no matter what
it is. Success, peace, health, love. You name it, it does not
matter. The only thing that matters is that you believe, even
when it comes to integrity and discipline as a Christian.

In truth, the life of Christ is a disciplined life — a life
based on self-control and self-restraint. The power to do this
comes from the Holy Ghost Who is on the inside of you.
He is powerful enough to make whatever you are believing
God to do, or to do in God, come to pass. The Holy Ghost
is in you to help you live a life of integrity, among the other
virtues that show Christ within. The Holy Ghost is a gift
of help and enablement. He is not, as some Christians feel,
a nuisance or a problem. If anyone is, it is us, not God. We
are the ones who need the work done on us, not the other
way around. We should spend more time working on us
and not trying to change the Holy Ghost to suit us. Doing
so will solve the problem of missing integrity in the Church.
Needless to say, without the Holy Ghost, integrity is not
in us. At least, not as God desires and gives it. If integrity
is lacking, other virtues important to the Lord's service suffer.
A main one is the discipline.

Discipline is a product of the presence of the Holy Spirit.
His being there automatically supplies what the Church
needs to discipline herself. But many Christians do not want
to submit to what the Spirit provides for self-control and
self-restraint. While they may enjoy going around talking
about having the Holy Ghost, they deny His power in
themselves by not manifesting godly discipline. Rather than

submit to it, and demonstrate it, they choose to speak against
it, saying that discipline is a
**Discipline is a** carryover of legalism and, there-
**product of the** fore, should be shunned rather
**presence of the** than cultivated. To avoid the greatly
**Holy Spirit.** feared taboo of legalism, they give
license to the flock of the Lord to
go ahead and fulfill the lusts of the flesh.

God, however, frowns on this. He is looking for
disciples, followers of His Son, who diligently practice being
as He is. How can you genuinely be a disciple of Christ
without being as He is? The very meaning of the word *disciple*
implies discipline. For sure, it does not come easy, but
discipline is very much a minimal requirement for a disciple
of Jesus Christ, particularly in view of the fact that it is
unnatural to be disciplined. It is a trait that must be
developed.

Natural man has a hard time with this. His basic nature
hates discipline because he hates obedience, and obedience
is what comes out of discipline. He hates it because he is
independent. He prides himself on his ability to stand on
his own two feet and do things his own way. Every intelligent
person, even the littlest child, finds his delight in doing
things his own way. It is common to man and easy for the
old nature. Why? Because man hates authority. He hates
being told what to do. As quickly as he can, he breaks away
from authority in favor of his own course in life. No matter
what it costs him or what the risk, he simply has to do things
on his own. It is the spirit of the world, and the same spirit
is creeping into and taking hold in the Church.

But you don't have to fall prey to it. When your heart
is after God, He will supply all your needs according to His
riches in glory and you do not have to fear His abuse,
oppression or anything else in return for it. Proverbs tells
us that the Lord makes rich and adds no sorrow to it. (Prov.
10:22.) Jeremiah tells us that God's intentions toward us are
good and not evil, to give us a future and a hope. Therefore,

you do not have to fear being obedient or submissive to Him

**He has your best
interests at heart.**
because the scripture shows you
that He has your best interests at
heart. So focus on Jesus, set your
attention on His integrity and let it
reign in your life. And do it with godly motives, because
wrong motives will never do the job. In the long run, they
will backfire.

Set your heart to see how much hope there is for you
in relationship to the Holy Spirit and your spirit and watch
integrity grow in you and you along with it.

# 5

# The Power of Integrity

Integrity is learned. It is not showered on you, nor are you naturally born with it. To develop it, you have to work at it. It takes many things, consistency, honesty, purity of heart and a constant effort to build **Love will never fail** an impressive practice of integrity. **to inspire integrity.** Over time it will grow strong, and you will discover one day that you have earned yourself a measure of authority as a result of steadily working on, and maintaining, a respectable life of integrity. Oh, and it takes love, too. Love for God and love for His people. People will always respond to love, and love will never fail to inspire integrity — a lesson many preachers would do well to learn.

Far too many preachers today are in major competition for power and authority. They manipulate, coerce and exploit to prove their authority is real, or that they have any real authority at all. Neglecting the cultivation of the respect that assures authority, they rival one another for it, foolishly. This is unfortunate since people are simply not as stupid as such actions would indicate they are. They know power and they know authority. When they meet a preacher who really has authority, they will know it, and no amount of competition in the world could cause them not to know the difference. It is better to rely on your integrity to bring the rewards of fame, authority and honor. Like every other merit in life, it has to be earned. If you want people to start looking up to you and taking you serious, no matter what office you hold, you need to apply the principles of integrity. Then you won't have to horse whip them into obedience or respect.

I laid hold of this truth early in my service to God. I remember back in September, 1990, my team and I had our first major crusade in the capital city of Lusaka. A stadium was chosen for the crusade and things were smoothly running along. Unexpectedly, a lady came to see me during the time, and said, "The President has been wanting to meet with you." Three months before, our country had experienced its first (and worst) food riots. The situation in the country was tense. The push was on for a multi-party system of government, and as a result, everything was unusually sensitive. The Church, because of the tension, was careful in what she said for fear of intimidation. I said to the lady who came to me, "If the President needs me, he will definitely call me." The President at the time was Dr. Kenneth Kaunda who had been in office for twenty-seven years.

The following day, I received a call from the secretary to the cabinet that he wanted to come with his family for prayer at the guest house. I agreed, and he did. When they arrived, I prayed with the family and they were gloriously filled with the power of the Holy Ghost. Afterward, I wanted to find out if the President still wanted to see me. That evening I got my answer. A call came in telling me I had to be at the State House at 8:00 the next morning. One of my associates drove with me to meet the President for the first time — officially.

We were welcomed warmly by everyone and were quickly whisked into a waiting room. On the way we silently asked God for His supernatural wisdom. When we were called in, the thick double doors were closed behind us, and President Kaunda stretched his hand out to greet. After we were seated, God's miracle began. The anointing of God came upon me and I could feel it. As I studied the President I saw that he looked thin and weary. Things were taking their toll on him and it was showing. At the height of the opposition he was facing, I saw he was a lonely man. Breaking the short silence, he started by saying, "I've been wanting to meet with you since you began the crusade early this week, but I have been extremely busy. Looking at him, I knew he wanted to be open and freely share his hurts and fears, so I began with what God had given me early that morning during my prayer time. It was the story of the "Rich Young Ruler."

I responded to him by saying, "Sir, God is not able to help you until you surrender your life and give up any fetishes that could be around the State House." I dealt with his involvement in Eastern religions. My reply was based on Mark 10:17-21, which reads,

> **And when he was gone forth into the way, there came one running, and kneeled to him, and asked him, Good Master, what shall I do that I may inherit eternal life? And Jesus said unto him, Why callest thou me good? There is none good but one, that is, God. Thou knowest the commandments, do not commit adultery, do not kill, do not steal, do not bear false witness, defraud not, honour thy father and mother. And he answered and said unto him, Master, all these have I observed from my youth. Then Jesus beholding him loved him, and said unto him, One thing thou lackest: go thy way, sell whatsoever thou hast, and give to the poor, and thou shalt have treasure in heaven: and come, take up the cross, and follow me.**

Jesus said to the rich young ruler, **One thing thou lackest**. I said to the President, "Jesus will help you by saving you from your sins. You have to give up your faith in other gods and trust only Jesus for salvation." An altar call was made and the response was immediate. The President climbed down from his seat and knelt down in front of me to honor and receive Jesus Christ into his heart. We joined hands and had a glorious time of prayer. He repeated the sinner's prayer after me just like in the crusades.

My associate was watching all this, amazed at my boldness and the President's response, and the presence of the Holy Spirit in the room. Little did I know that in two hours time the President was going to address the nation on radio and television to diffuse a political time bomb, one that could have brought untold bloodshed to Zambia. He declared Zambia a multi-party state.

Integrity brings trust. The kind that signals to troubled souls it is safe to reach out. People and leaders alike need to know who can help them in times of crises. Although they may appear to differ with you in public, inside their hearts they register for future use **Integrity brings** who is genuine. Integrity of this **trust.** sort doesn't fail to give you authority. God repeated this miracle a second time, twenty-one days after the new President, Mr. F.T.J. Chiluba came to power. I had a meeting with him. What a difference it made to meet a man who was not just a president, but a brother in the Lord, too. When we met, he stretched out his hands and shouted, "Brother Nevers." We spent time together over lunch, and in the evening we shared from God's Word. It was rich. Oh, what joy I felt to see a president pray in the Spirit with me for a long time. At the memory of this event, I recall Proverbs 18:16 which says, **A man's gift maketh room for him, and bringeth him before great men.** These fond memories settled for me once and for all the blessedness of walking in integrity, and I don't take lightly the responsibilities that go along with it.

I made up my mind a long time ago never to speak against any man of God, and to never respond to the press. These two principles together have helped to build and sustain the level of integrity I need to get God's business done. Without them and the power of integrity, I am sure there can be no lasting revival anywhere.

## Influencing A Nation for God

Daniel came from a godly background, accustomed to the synagogue, the Law and the fear of God.

He was captured together with Hananiah, Mishael, and Azariah, whose names were later changed by Nebuchadnezzar to Shadrach, Meshach and Abednego.

They were brought to the pagan, ungodly nation of Babylon. The culture was different. It was that of indulgence. You were not only expected to indulge, but it was almost demanded of you to conform and be like everybody else. The latest was to be like everybody else. Indulgence stemmed from pride. To succeed, one was to indulge in extravagant eating, exotic dressing and anything that exalts and gratifies the flesh. Naturally, the greatest pressure was on the young people. They had to prove their manhood. In a land where God's Spirit is absent, substitutes are sought to satisfy man. Great dances and night clubs are all futile quests to find satisfaction in a land devoid of God's Spirit. The other obvious aspect of this society is that they lived to impress their king. To them, Nebuchadnezzar was the absolute authority. If he invited you to a state function, it made you feel like you had reached human's height of desire! More like God is to them that seek Him.

It was more against this backdrop that Daniel and his friends had to contend for their faith in Israel's God, Jehovah. When they landed in Babylon, they had two obvious choices. First choice, to conform and join the fun. At least rules didn't exist there when it came to morality. They had no law of Moses. Pressure was definitely on the four young men.

The second choice was almost the unnecessary one — to transform. To transform an already set, powerful culture, was the road they chose to tread. In choosing the road of self-dignity, they decided to change the culture rather than the culture changing them. Daniel and his friends decided not to indulge in either the free morality of the land or the worship of Nebuchadnezzar. The penalty faced in both of these cases was nothing less than death. The book of Daniel reveals the courage of the young people who said no to a rundown culture, and yes to God.

Here is what I want you to see. Because they stood tall for God in the midst of opposition, to the point of looking stupid, God stood for them. HE REVEALED HIMSELF TO THEM. Whenever you stand for God in a broken-down society, God reveals Himself to you. Notice how God revealed the meaning of Nebuchadnezzar's dream to Daniel. The Bible doesn't tell us that before Daniel decided to stand for God, he had a ministry of dream interpretation, but when he challenged the spirit of the age, in Babylon, God started to speak to him immediately. The result is amazing. After the interpretation of the dream, Nebuchadnezzar fell down before Daniel to worship him, and then honored him by giving him authority in running the affairs of the land. In other words, Nebuchadnezzar said, transform our culture, because your God is the God of gods. Change the nation was the king's cry.

**Whenever you stand for God in a broken-down society, God reveals Himself to you.**

Another story in the New Testament parallels Daniel's victory. It is where Stephen in Acts 6 and 7 radically spoke for God in the midst of great tension and danger. The penalty for this stand was also death, which Stephen got. However, in principle, God's revelation of Himself to Stephen was similar to Daniel. The Bible says Stephen saw heaven opened and saw the Son of Man standing on the right hand of the Father. (Acts 7:56.) I believe that anyone who chooses to stand for God in a torn-down society receives a standing ovation from heaven. The Bible says in Romans 8:34, Jesus Christ is sitting at the right hand of the Father in heaven. I believe that as Stephen was getting ready to enter heaven, Jesus stood to give a hero's welcome to a man who was ready to stand up for Jesus in the midst of an indulgent generation. When you stand up for God, God stands up for you.

**When you stand up for God, God stands up for you.**

We must change our culture to that of the fear of God. That's really what revival is all about. To influence an ugly culture is to bring in a new culture — one full of the fear of God.

# 6

# Integrity and the Holy Spirit

How does the baptism of the Holy Ghost affect the subject of integrity? There was a teaching going around during the early days of my conversion that said once you received the baptism of the Holy Ghost, all your character traits are brought under God's control automatically, without any effort on the part of the believer whatsoever. Positively, this is not so.

In this chapter, I will throw more light on this view and the Biblical revelation of the work of the Holy Spirit. It clearly says, **You shall receive power** (not integrity), **after that the Holy Ghost is come upon you** (Acts 1:8). You are qualified to receive the Holy Ghost the moment you get saved. It is the promised power from on high spoken of by Jesus during His last days with the disciples. A gift from God, the Holy Ghost is an enablement that empowers you to live out the Christ life in faith and in victory.

The Holy Ghost basically does two things for you. First, He gives you power to resist the enemy (Satan) which you cannot hope to successfully do in the flesh. Second, the Holy Ghost gives you power to demonstrate the power of God. You actually start to move in the abilities of God, known as the supernatural. When the Spirit of God comes upon you, the sick are healed and the Gospel is preached with power so that the great results of salvation take place.

Another good example of the work of the Holy Spirit is that of Peter in the Upper Room. Once he was gloriously filled, he preached his first Holy Ghost-inspired and fortified sermon. It was so powerful that it found a place in the very ranks of scripture up to this day. Peter was changed by the experience from an unstable fisherman to a Holy Ghost preacher who moved souls to salvation's repentance and conversion. Still, with all that, notice that while he had the Holy Ghost, it did not stop him from being accused a little later of racial bias by Paul when they were ministering among the Galatians.

That passage strongly makes my point. True, the Holy Ghost is a gift from God. It is freely **Integrity must be** given and requires no action on the **learned and then** part of the receiver other than faith. **developed.** However, integrity is an entirely different matter. It must be learned and then developed. Hence, it requires effort and that means work.

Integrity has to do with bringing the flesh under subjection. We have many examples of powerful preachers who have affected our generation whose characters turned out to be totally undesirable. Something not too uncommon in any generation, for history records character flaws have been the ruin of many a great example. Little habits, fetishes or compulsions spoil an otherwise potent witness. They lie, smoke, are unfaithful to their spouses and a number of other things. Yet, with all this, they still seem to be moving under the anointing of the Holy Ghost. Remarkably, God continues to bear witness to them even though they have all manner of uncleanness and sin lurking in the background of their lives. Why? How does one explain this?

By one fundamental premise. Gifts and callings are not character and morals, nor do they constitute them in ministry. A person's ministry is not to be merited on the ground of their charisma, or the miracles they demonstrate. Performance is not related to quality in this case. What it takes for a person to be used of God as opposed to what it takes for a person to exemplify God are two different things. Therefore, it should be on the ground of a minister's character and integrity that a person is judged and his service is evaluated. The proper mixture of the baptism of the Holy Ghost and integrity together brings the character needed to influence a generation. Once you receive the baptism of the Holy Ghost, the seed for integrity is planted. It is then up to you to bring forth the fruit of the Spirit. You do so by constantly watering the ground of the heart, and pruning of the fruit of the seed sown. The Bible calls the product of this action the fruit of the Spirit. Fruit, as you well know, takes time to grow, naturally and spiritually. To be strong and lasting, trees, for example, need constant attention to produce the best yield. If proper care is not taken, fruit may grow for a season or two, but eventually poor care will cause the fruit to go bad, and over time, the tree's production of fruit will quit.

**Performance is not related to quality.**

The same is true with the Charismatic Movement. We need both fire and character to last. The baptism of the Holy Ghost gives us the fire while the fruit of the Spirit gives us the character. We need both to continue with ministry. God is looking for fruit that abides. True power of ministry is character more than fire.

While the baptism of the Holy Ghost is for your personal power and fire, the fruit of the Spirit is for the world's consumption. Just as the fruit on the apple tree is not produced for the apple tree to enjoy, neither is the fruit of the Spirit for the saint to enjoy himself. Numerous Charismatics have spent time comparing their tongues instead of producing fruit for the world. Real revival goes beyond improved tongues to character of the tongue talker. Jesus said, "The devil has no part in Me," because He knew He walked in integrity. David said, **Search me, O God, and know my heart: try me and know my thoughts** (Psalm 139:23).

Another misconception exists as far as the salvation message is concerned. For the longest time, I believed that once Jesus saves you, then the devil couldn't touch you anymore. This is also not so. When you give yourself to God, all hell turns against you. James puts it clearly, **. . . Receive with meekness the engrafted word, which is able to save your souls** (James 1:21). The truth is when you get saved, your spirit man is renewed and born again, but your mind is not. It is a bank whose deposits consist of all your former life and activities. Peter teaches in his epistles that the believer is born again, but his mind is not. Our mind must be saved too (or renewed) by getting the Word of God into our system. The Bible calls the Word of God the water of the Word. As you drink in Gods Word, your mind is being cleansed from all filth and dirt. Only the Word of God can do this which tells us where the Charismatic crisis lies. We are saved, filled with the Holy Ghost but are involved in an intense moral battle.

**We are involved in an intense moral battle.**

The question asked by many young men is, "Why am I experiencing such wild sex drives when I am saved and filled with the Holy Ghost?" Well, the truth is that your soul (mind) is not yet regenerated. It needs to be taught how to behave by your receiving of the Word of God. In our quest for victory over the enemy, let us not forget our code of discipline which is the Word that teaches us how not to yield to the pulls and tugs of the flesh.

It is important for each one of us to realize that we are not supernatural. We need protection from the enemy. The Bible says, **Flee also youthful lusts. . .** (2 Timothy 2:22). The word *flee* means to run as in terror. Do not overestimate your resistance power. Many saved, Holy Ghost-filled people believe they can resist any temptation. That's a lie. Being filled with the Holy Ghost doesn't mean you are no longer human with red blood flowing through your veins. You do not become superhuman. So when tempted to sin, flee. For only then will God's grace be sufficient for you.

To illustrate, Joseph was a young man of integrity. He loved God and was totally dedicated to God. But when Potiphar's wife wanted to jump on him, Joseph did not start talking in tongues to scare the woman away. He could have started to move in the gifts of the Spirit, but this was not the time for any of that. Instead, it was time to move with his feet. He fled. His attitude promoted him. Integrity brings promotion.

# 7

# The Charismatic Crisis

In this chapter, I want to address the other side of the Gospel of Jesus Christ. That is that God is holy and anything unholy provokes His wrath. The Bible says we must keep the full counsel of God. It is true that our God is a God of love and the God of compassion, but He's also a God of wrath. There are two sides of God.

One day as I was meditating, I wondered about the state of the Church. I asked the Lord why there is so much sin, pride, moral breakdown and lack of discipline among the Charismatics and Pentecostals of our day. Now when I mention Charismatics, I'm referring to the new work that God is doing all over the world. My motive is not denominational because I know Heaven is not going to be full of Baptists, Pentecostals or Charismatics. Heaven is going to be full of people who have been washed by the blood of Jesus Christ and who follow Him. Church affiliation does not matter, only that you've come to Jesus and He has washed you in His blood — even if you are Catholic. Jesus is, by the way, doing something among the Catholics today. Sometimes I think there might be more Catholics in Heaven than Pentecostals. When Catholics get hold of God, they hold on with their dear life. With us Pentecostals, it is different. We are too used to God, too familiar with Him. So much so that the fear of God has left our lives, making us treat God like our cousin.

I want you to understand that I believe the Charismatic and Pentecostal Movements have made one of the biggest spiritual impacts on our day. There has been a renewed

53

interest in the Word of God because of them. Charismatic believers are spending hours on their knees and on their faces worshipping God. Through them prayer has come alive. The whole face of Christianity is changing in the hands of the Charismatics today. No longer is God being treated as just a mere religion; He is now vividly seen as a Person. Christianity, in truth, never was a religion, but a relationship with a Person: the Person Jesus Christ. In our generation, however, the Charismatic and Pentecostal Movements are under fire. We are under attack. Even though we are born again and filled with the Holy Spirit, our actions have become ugly.

Our old ways are slipping back into our lives and we are falling prey to much of our old sin. You wonder how a born-again Christian can do such things as backslide in their conduct. Do you wonder why it is that when you want to walk right, the devil always gets you even though you are born again? Do you find it frustrating to know you are born again, washed in the blood, but somehow the devil still seems to get access to you?

Last year God gave me a thought on these questions. Simply stated, the devil is after the good people — the saved ones. Meanwhile, God is after the bad ones — the sinners. Jesus takes the sinners and makes them good. The devil attacks the good ones to make them bad. It is a furious battle. If you don't bother the devil or give him any trouble, you are not going to have any trouble from him. Yet, when you start to follow God and make up your mind to be different, to spend time in prayer on your knees and get the Word of God in your spirit and dedicate your life to God, then know for sure that all hell is going to break loose against you. That happens purely because the devil hates those who are strong in God. The stronger you are in the Lord, the more trouble you are going to have from the devil. The Bible tells us in Psalms 34:19 **Many are the afflictions of the righteous: but the Lord delivereth him out of them all.**

Many are the afflictions of the righteous, but the Lord delivers him out of them all. Saint Paul said when he had the thorn in the flesh, he prayed three times to God. In essence he said, "Lord, remove it from me." But God answered by saying essentially, "Son, My grace shall be sufficient for you." Like Paul, you too may be going through trouble but know the grace of God is sufficient for you, meaning it is more than enough to console your pain. Don't doubt God has seen your tears, your troubles and the pain you bear. Just know that He says, "My child, no matter what you go through, My grace is sufficient for you." Jesus told us that in this world we shall have tribulation, but in the face of it, to be of good cheer. Why? Because Jesus has overcome the world.

**The grace of God is sufficient for you.**

Yes, trouble will come, but His grace is all that is needed to go through the fire. The devil is after the righteous which is why they have trouble in the flesh with him. The Charismatics, therefore, are high targets of Satan's attacks. The Charismatic Movement has inspired many routine Christians to catch the flames of God. They have turned the mundane Church world inside out. It follows, reasonably, that they should defend themselves by waging a good warfare and guarding themselves spiritually more than any other group. They cannot afford to allow their weaknesses to be their ruin.

Why is there so much sin among the Charismatics and Pentecostals? One case will help me make my point. Once I heard about a prominent minister of God who fell into sin. One reporter covering the fall said on television that he was a phony and a hypocrite. On the surface that may appear so, but it does not have to be the truth. A look at the record of such a minister could show he undoubtedly loved God and knew God, and as a result, was shaking the kingdom of darkness. The eyes of the devil were certainly on him. His very work made him an open target for Satan's onslaughts. Incidents like these tell you who are the people in trouble with the devil — preachers, men and women who love God and are devoted to His work. They are prime targets of the devil.

When you are doing something for God, the devil puts the spotlight on you and says, "Get him from God." The Bible says that the eyes of the Lord are upon the righteous. (1 Peter 3:12.) True, the devil is looking at you, trying to trick you. Jesus' eyes are upon you today and always.

Another reason why there is so much trouble among Pentecostals is their misconception about the new birth in Jesus Christ. To best understand this, I need to explain what it is to be born again. When you realize you are a sinner, you receive Jesus into your heart. The Spirit of God moves on your dead spirit and your spirit is made alive. All of a sudden, your spirit is regenerated, born again, made new. Your desires change as a result, as does your taste in friends, conversation and living. This happens because your spirit is new and is now alive to God and dead to sin. When God speaks from this time on, you say, "Yes, Lord, my ears are open." Your spiritual eyes are open. You are born again. But it is only your spirit. The rest of you — your soul and your body — has to be changed little by little to answer the whole sin problem.

Man is made up of three parts: spirit, soul and body. When your spirit is born again, your body is not. Your soul and your mind also are not born again. Here is where the problem of Charismatic and Pentecostal sin comes in. We jump around with the helmet of salvation on and nothing else. No sword of the Spirit is in our hands or any of the other spiritual armor we need to fend off the wiles of the devil. While there is no question about your salvation, you are saved and alive to God, but if you lack the other spiritual things you need to survive that don't come automatically with salvation, you cannot hope to stand up under the devil's pressure.

The new birth is only the beginning and it is spiritual. Outward changes don't happen. Suppose you had a scar on

your face before you became a Christian. After you are born
again, the scar will still be there. Your body stays the same
on the outside, but your spirit, on the other hand, becomes
a new man. Yes, from then on,
Jesus sees the new man of your
spirit, but the old man of the soul
is not saved immediately. To sur-
vive the devil's tricks, you need to make some outside
changes. Your mind, for one thing, needs to be renewed to
the things of God. You have to clean up your thoughts and
get the mind of God. One of the problems is the mind. The
Word of God says whoever controls your mind is the lord
of your life. Don't forget to give the Lord control of your
mind.

**The new birth is
only the beginning.**

It is your mind that becomes the battlefield for God and
the enemy. Whoever has your thought life and your will
controls you. James says, **Receive with meekness the
engrafted word, which is able to save your souls** (James
1:21). He is talking to believers, to Christians. He is telling
them to get the Word of God and to meditate on it. The Word
is the water that washes the mind and removes all the filth
of the world and the old nature so the enemy will have no
hold over you. This process is what is needed to make your
mind line up with your spirit and the Spirit of God in you.

Since your spirit is born again and your mind is not,
there is always a battle between your flesh and spirit, a battle
that will surely make your commitment to integrity a difficult
one. The two will ever be at enmity with one another as
Romans and Galatians teach. When God speaks to Nevers
Mumba to give $200 to my brother, I hear it in my spirit
because my spirit is alive to God. When God speaks, my
spirit understands since God is Spirit. (John 4:24.) When
God says to my spirit, "Give $200 to Brother Rynaldo. Please
give it now," my spirit is excited and I want to give. Then
the unsaved mind says, "Ah-oh! Wait a minute; just wait a
minute. Does it really make sense for you to give him so
much money? Who is he to you anyway?"

Meanwhile, your spirit is saying, "Give him, give, him give him, give him." The voice of your mind, though, is louder than your spirit. It is this way because for so many years before you were born again, it was your boss. So you are more attuned to the voice of your mind than the voice of your spirit. The mind's voice says, "Don't do it. Youve got to pay your water bill; you've got to pay the electricity bill. You will starve and die from hunger."

If you have been feeding on God's Word, you will recognize suddenly there is a battle between your spirit and your mind. Here is where you decide not to give in to your mind and not to grieve the Holy Spirit Who has spoken to you. The Word of God in you lets God speak to your spirit and the message goes to your mind causing an agreement to occur between the two. Now you no longer hesitate to pull out the checkbook and write a check to your brother Rynaldo. You know if God is telling you to do that, it should be done right now and He will be very happy. Amen.

In the Charismatic and Pentecostal world, far too often we do not hide the Word of God in our hearts. Hence, when the Holy Spirit speaks, there is frequently no agreement between Him and the mind. Jesus told a story about the sower who goes out to sow. The Bible says some seeds fell on stony ground. The roots went to some distance and the plant came up. The seed was all right. The story pictures the trials of life. When the temptations and afflictions came, these plants could not stand because their roots were not deep enough. Such is the case with most Charismatics and Pentecostals. Not hiding Gods Word in their hearts keeps them from hearing and obeying the Lord. Many of you — and this is not a prophecy — if you won't stand later in life, if you don't change your minds now. There is a day coming of real tribulation, that the Bible foretells is the coming of a shaking, a mighty shaking, within the Body of Christ. The only people who shall stand are those who have their roots grounded in God and His Word. When the winds blow, a tree will move and sway but remains grounded and unable to fall. So it is with Christians who bury God's Word within. It will keep them in the day of trial and tribulations.

My roots are in God, in the Word of God. My roots are not just in experience, nor are they only in tongues. But my roots are in the Word of God. The Bible says this world will pass away. It will perish, but the Word of God shall never perish. His Word shall remain forever. Not a jot or a tittle shall remain unfulfilled in the Word of God. To the people of the Charismatic and Pentecostal Movements, I give this challenge: If you want to make it in these last days, get the Word of God into your spirit. Embrace the Word of God because when your money goes, when your friends go, when your hair disappears, your human integrity fails, the Word of God shall remain strong in your life. Therefore, remain with the Word of God. Gather it, eat it, put it on the inside of your heart that you may not sin. When everything fails, then the Word of God shall sustain you.

**My roots are in the Word of God.**

**Get the Word of God into your spirit.**

# 8

# Integrity and Charismatic Witchcraft

The story of Cain and Abel in Genesis 4 never ceases to amaze me. Within this account lies the description of man's heart once it became darkened by sin. Man's heart is continually evil until the light of Christ is shed abroad in it. Why did Cain kill his own brother? How could he kill his own brother when something like murder was, up to that point, unheard of. To answer, we must turn to our text and explore the Genesis account a bit more. Look at the highlights of the incident:

1. Both Cain and Abel offered their sacrifices to God.

2. Abel's was accepted and Cain's was rejected.

3. Cain was offended.

4. Cain still deceitfully talked to his brother.

5. Cain, in his envy, rose up and slew his brother.

Let's delve into this a little deeper.

It is highly probable that before the sacrifices were offered, normal brotherly love existed between Cain and Abel. The moment ministry to God came in, fighting and murder came in. Since this incident is brought out in the book of beginnings, Genesis, Bible scholars call it the "Principle of the First Mention," meaning, all similar recurrences of this event should be interpreted by the first occurrence.

Expanding on this, the first of human treachery and tragedy, the Bible says, **The heart is deceitful above all things, and desperately wicked: who can know it?** (Jeremiah 17:9). The Genesis account reveals that Cain's offering was rejected, the basis of which was purely God's own judgment. God, knowing the intent of man's heart, sees what man can never see. His searching of the hearts of the two men provided His reasons for rejecting Cain's sacrifice. The event, however, if viewed perceptively, brought in the very inception of the witchcraft spirits of envy and jealousy.

Envy and jealousy were the motivations behind Cain's hateful act. It started in his heart with his bitter resentment of God's acceptance of Abel's offering and rejection of his own. Here lies the root of today's problem within the Charismatic Movement — envy and bitter resentment. Cain wondered why Abel's sacrifice would be accepted and not his. He brooded over it day and night until he concluded the problem would be settled if his **Here lies the root of today's problem within the Charismatic Movement — envy and bitter resentment.** brother no longer existed. The answer was simple — his brother would have to die. Though unheard of before, something in Cain told him that he could remove his brother from the earth. Something inside him said all he had to do was strike him with a fatal blow, shed his blood and his God-approved brother would forever cease to be.

Cain's distorted thinking was natural. It was the basic thinking in the heart of man. Go through scripture with me for a moment, as we further explore this attitude. We will start with the story of Joseph in Genesis 37. Joseph was loved by his father more than the rest of his brothers. The result of his father's imbalanced affection was favoritism. The brothers, understandably, reacted with resentment. They too saw the solution as murder. Kill the favored son and the father would have more place in his heart for them. They devised a plot to take the young man's life, but God had other plans. He intervened and preserved Joseph alive. Instead, the Lord arranged for Joseph to be sold as a slave, an act that led to his becoming Egypt's prime minister.

What did Joseph do wrong to cause his brothers to have such malice toward him? Joseph did nothing except to be the favored and most beloved of his father. His brothers hoped that by killing the boy they would get their fair share of their father's love. Again, this was distorted thinking, but it is man's basic thinking, the only way he knows to handle hostile conflicts and rivalry. History repeats itself again and again.

Another case is David, the sweet psalmist of Israel. The Bible calls him, "a man after God's own heart." He found favor in God's sight. After an extraordinary successful war victory, the women of the land sang David's praise. Innocently, they rejoiced over the young man's slaughter of the tens of thousands with the jawbone of an ass. Saul heard their praise. Why, they were giving glory to another, the king thought. He brooded over and despised David for his success. The brooding took hold, and an unclean spirit overcame him. He wanted David dead. From that moment on, the resentful king sought every opportunity to take David's life. The spirit of envy that stalked him consumed him and venomous hatred seized his heart toward David.

Throughout the Bible this envious spirit is seen as king after king, leader after leader, is obsessed with the destruction of a rival or brother. I call it, "the spirit of Cain." It entered Saul and countless others down through the years. Saul failed to destroy God's man David. Nevertheless, he still ended up in witchcraft, which brings us to the account of his meeting with the witch of En-dor in I Samuel 28:7. The story of the witch at En-dor illustrates the outcome of "the Cain spirit." We in the modern Church often contend with the same spirit.

Charismatic ministers have succumbed to "the Cain Spirit." They have abandoned their ministry posts of duty in pursuit of the murder (spiritually speaking) of their brethren. They rise up in malice against another minister because he seems to be getting all the attention. Let's face **Charismatic ministers have succumbed to "the Cain spirit."** it. When you hear a fellow preacher preach with power and precision, are you blessed or resentful of the success of your colleague? The answer determines your link to the Cain/Saul response to another's good fortune. If envy is your reaction, then you are in danger of falling into what I call Charismatic witchcraft. I have noticed this kind of witchcraft is strongest with those we know, our kinsmen and brothers. With Cain, it was the same way. His hatred was directed toward his own brother. Modern Cains struggle with similar emotion. Distant ministers don't raise such threatening feelings in us, only those nearby. In fact, the distant ones are often our heroes. Rarely are we intimidated by preachers from other countries. Therefore, they pose no real threat to us. The preacher next door, though, is another thing.

He is a real threat because he is there with us in competition for the same souls we are after. His church may be bigger, he's driving his own car, his wife is pretty and prayerful, people are speaking well of his work, and not saying much, if anything at all, about yours. A situation like this sparks the beginning of Charismatic witchcraft. We have all been attacked by the temptations of this hideous spirit at one time or another. Man naturally wants to be the only hero in his own world. Even so, we must yield to the Spirit of God and not our own flesh.

My prayer to God for the present Charismatic Movement is that the "performance spirit," the potent stronghold that breeds rivalry, be destroyed. I am talking about the one that measures success only by results. It says, results and only results are important.

A while back, our Crusade Team had just ended a seven-day crusade in the country of Botswana. God had performed wonderful miracles of salvation and healing. A couple afterward invited the entire team to lunch. While we ate and talked, we delved into the ministries of various preachers around the world. Then our hostess started to testify. She innocently mentioned the name of a pastor in West Africa whom she thought was the greatest preacher she ever heard. She was sitting opposite me and her statement pierced my heart like a sharp arrow for two reasons. One was that I knew the preacher myself and was aware of his extremely successful ministry. Second, I had been preaching every night in the crusade, and it was as if she was saying, "I heard you preach, but I know someone who can really preach." At that moment, I had to deal with "the Cain spirit" vehemently. I almost thought I heard the women in the days of Saul saying, "Saul has killed his thousands, but David his ten thousands." What a challenge! My general manager looked at me and made the comment that revealed the torment of his heart. He said to me quietly, not in the hearing of our hostess, "Hey, I believe we are also great preachers."

Battles like these are fought daily. It is the same among musicians who cannot stand other musicians. If one sings well, they start to wish his equipment would blow up or that they would get a mild heart attack It sounds terrible, but that is how desperately wicked the heart of man can be. Oh, we don't say it, but it can sometimes be our earnest wish. I am calling this Charismatic witchcraft. If you struggle with these symptoms, you need deliverance.

Witchcraft is not the collection of herbs and fetishes people think of when the Word is heard. It is expressions, spiritual expressions, of the Satanic adamic man who feels endangered by anything that does not give him preeminence and glory. Here is an example. Spiritually speaking, your fetish (an instrument or charm used to achieve an unclean supernatural effect) could be your tongue. With it you can kill another minister of God by speaking evil of him. So serious is this to God that He commanded Israel not to speak evil of the ruler of her people.

James sternly warns us about the unruliness of the tongue and the fierce fire it can kindle with words. Solomon in the book of Proverbs repeatedly admonishes us about the perils and pleasures ignited by the tongue. Envy and jealousy kindle all sorts of negative spiritual acts with but a word. How many times have you heard about a prominent minister being slandered by vicious rumors and accusations from fellow believers once his ministry took off? For sure, when this happens, the rumors will begin to fly.

Suddenly you will hear that the founder's life is loose, his marriage is unstable, he loves money or other such things to turn the people's head from his work to idle imaginations. Accusations like these will always be there because they have proven over the centuries to **Lay down your pride** be powerful enough to destroy any **and refuse to** minister. How do you resist the **become a witch of** spirit of witchcraft in these cases? **accusation.** Start by blessing these ministers instead of cursing the work of their hands. Pray that God accepts it. Thank God for their ministry service, and then go to Him to help. Lay down your pride and refuse to become a witch of accusation.

The fruit of the Spirit must be predicted. The Bible makes it clear that you can't curse what God has blessed. My heart yearns for my generation when it comes to this, for its vast potential and the obstacles to releasing it are hindered by those who fall prey to Charismatic witchcraft. Needless to say, integrity falters in the face of such obstacles. The only way integrity can flourish is when the confidence and security of the Lord Jesus Christ are reigning again in the Church and when the vessels of His habitation submit to it.

Don't be intimidated by another man's success. Be a David instead of a Saul. David said, **Search me O God, and know my heart: try me, and know my thoughts** (Psalm 139:23). The only way to overcome is to face your symptoms and hostilities of witchcraft and diffuse them with love. You may not have what the next preacher has, but you are on your way to victory. Since you have your particular race to run, run it with truth, love and patience. Be accountable, make yourself answerable to God and man.

One area where accountability is shaky is in the area of finances. Integrity must spill over in the area of finances to restore the people's trust in the ministers of God. Integrity means accountability. That is, dealing honestly before both God and man. One of the most **The greatest** sensitive areas on the subject of **challenge to a** personal integrity is that of money **servant of God is** and accountability. Too many **finances.** ministers refuse to account for their handling of the Lord's money. The greatest challenge to a servant of God is finances. When a minister says he does not think about money, he either has no vision or he is a liar. Without money, you cannot so much as buy train tickets to carry the Gospel to the next point.

For us to maintain integrity in the area of finances, we first need to correct our attitude toward it. Admit the ministry demands money as an essential resource. Solomon said in Ecclesiastes, **Money answereth all things** (Eccles. 10:19b). Once you accept the importance of having money to do the work of the Lord, use your integrity to raise it according to the principles and plans of God for His Kingdom.

I have known pastors so fearful of challenging their congregation to give that they cry all night long because their personal and ministry needs are not being met. You must first accept that your need for money is real and godly. Upon doing so, the only thing that remains is that you come up with a God-approved strategy to obtain it. Get used to the fact that a constant major concern of ministry is that of finances. It will not go away, so deal with it boldly and wisely.

For example, to move our team and ministry equipment, advertise for the crusades through television, radio, news-papers and posters, it takes money. As long as we are to do it, it will take money. To hire stadiums and obtain other materials cost money, so we must, to continue our work, talk about money. It is no different with any minister of the Gospel.

When it comes to finances, the entire setup of most Third World ministries is a big joke. The way it goes is the pastors lead the congregation in praise and worship and collect the offering. They then preach a two-hour message. Afterward, they take the offering home and it becomes their ration for the week. Certainly this has no hint of integrity. Because of it many members are reluctant to give for fear of their hard-earned dollars being misused. In the end this practice becomes another assault on integrity.

Integrity speaks of accountability. Integrity means setting up a system with checks and balances that answers to others. Africa is going through a major shift in these areas.

**Integrity speaks of accountability.** Old beliefs about pastors, churches and finances are quickly being replaced. For the longest time, an African preacher was not to have money. The religious community dubbed it as evil. I grew up in a small Assembly of God Church where I served as an elder, and it was no different. Our policy was to keep our pastor under control by keeping his salary low. I have since repented of this evil and have asked forgiveness from the dear pastor who suffered much through our error. He is still doing a tremendous work for the Lord. Thank God.

It is the Church's responsibility to pay fair wages more than any other group in society. After all, if our covenant includes prosperity, as the Bible teaches, the only place the pastor, and other ministers can look to enjoy their share is the Church. The Church, the light of the world, is most heavily charged by God to have integrity and to be the standard of integrity to the world.

# 9

# Right Priorities Enhance Integrity

> Thus speaketh the Lord of hosts, saying, This people say, The time is not come, the time that the Lord's house should be built. Then came the word of the Lord by Haggai the prophet, saying, is it time for you, O ye, to dwell in your celled houses, and this house lie waste? Now therefore thus saith the Lord of hosts; Consider your ways.
>
> **Haggai 1:2-5**

God is calling us to think about our attitudes and priorities. (Read vs. 6.) It sounds very familiar to most of us. You may find yourself doing a few of these things: You sow much, but you do not get anything in return. You eat, but you are never full. You drink, but you are never filled with drink. You try to clothe yourself, but you are not warm. **Thus saith the Lord of hosts; consider your ways** (verse 7). Think about your ways. That is the first step toward setting right priorities, which enhances your integrity.

The best way for me to approach this subject is first to give you an understanding of the ministry of Haggai. We read a story about the man Haggai, standing up by the inspiration of God to challenge a generation that had begun well. Although Israel was devoted to God, her priority of putting God first shifted. In other words, the things of the world changed the priorities of the people of God. Though the Church and the children of Israel are two entirely different bodies, the Church

**The Church too has ceased to set its mind on the things above.**

too has ceased to set its mind on the things above and has begun to pursue the things of the world. The similarities between the two are staggering. Israel's history makes a perfect reference for our illustration.

The children of Israel were in captivity in Babylon for seventy years. When they were delivered from captivity, it was by the voice of God. God had spoken that after seventy years, they would be free from this captivity. The time was up and they were freed. They were free to rebuild the one thing they lacked in their captivity: a temple in which to worship God. To the Jewish people, the physical temple was like our physical bodies. It was the literal dwelling place of the Spirit of God. Spiritually speaking, our bodies are now the temple of the Holy Ghost. Then, it was a physical building that was needed to worship Jehovah, their God. In other words, they couldn't worship God to the fullest unless they had a temple because it represented the presence of God in their midst. As long as God was in their midst, they were happy, because they knew that all was well. Having Jehovah as their center was important to the Jewish people. Any exposure to their world will prove it.

Here is an example. I use many airlines to travel as we have many meetings in different parts of the world. One airline that really blessed me was the Israeli Airline. As soon as you land, many airlines pipe music through the intercom system by rock stars or people like that. However, what impressed me most was when we landed in an Israeli Airline jet, the music that came on was music about Jehovah. In the midst of all the hostility that surrounds it — three to four million people — surrounded by over a hundred million Arabs determined to crush them, Israel is still standing by the miracle hand of God. Why? Their allegiance to Jehovah. They are staunch preservers and defenders of their faith. For this reason, God said, "When I establish Jerusalem, I will establish it forever." Although Israel is not called a super power by the world, it is a super power with God. God stands for them. To get back to that theological discussion we started, here's what I'm saying.

Israel had just come out of captivity. They did not have a temple and yearned for one to serve their God. In prayer they most likely said many times, "Oh, God, take us back to Jerusalem so that we can rebuild Your house and worship You." The cry of their heart was to go back to Jerusalem and worship God one more time. God eventually released them to do so.

Once they went back to Jerusalem, one of their major tasks was to build the house of God. Without it, they were not secure from the enemy that surrounded them. God, they knew, was their only hope. Israel went back to Jerusalem with that as their priority, to build the temple of God. At first they started to build with zeal. At the beginning, they worked around the clock to build the temple of God. No sooner had they started to build when they were met with opposition. A group of Samaritans rose up to accuse them before the king of causing an insurrection. They reported the Jews were going to rise up against the kingdom of Cyrus and should be stopped. The plan worked. The Jews, as a result, stopped building.

Israel halted building the temple of God because of the opposition that was bringing trouble on them in the way of the trials that usually accompany obeying the Word of the Lord. The normal human response, to want to give up, is what they yielded to. How many times have we all felt like giving up? I know I have once, and again, it is not uncommon. Continue during those times when nobody understands you and everybody talks about you. Just keep your eyes fixed on God. He alone is the author and the finisher of your faith. God is the One Who called YOU, and He will be the One to help you too, and approve of you in front of the world and the Church.

**Just keep your eyes fixed on God.**

Don't wait for men to commend you. If you succeed in God, people are not always going to be happy that you are succeeding. Don't wait for people to slap you on the back.

Many times they won't. If you always look for the praise of men, you will never do the work of God. That is what this thing is all about — God, not man, God! Here is where Israel collapsed under the opposition of **Don't wait for men** men.
**to commend you.**
The nation was in a situation where they stopped building the temple of God because of opposition. Today's Israel can sympathize with them, especially in our country. The church in Zambia is largely at a crossroads, the same crossroads where Israel was. They rearranged their priorities and took their eyes off of God. Their fire had cooled and their zeal was gone. Many of you can relate to their problem.

Remember years ago when you first became born again, when you were on fire for the Lord? You witnessed to anything that moved. Anything that made a noise, you went and shared Jesus with it. You would have witnessed to a cat if it would give you five minutes. There was a desire burning within your bones and no devil could put it out. Your eyes were like a flame of fire. Every time you saw a person, you said to yourself, I wonder whether he knows Jesus? Do you remember those days when your heart was on fire for God? Israel had, according to Haggai, forgotten and had become lukewarm to the God Who had again delivered them from captivity. As a result, they gave in to the enemy and gave up the will of God for them.

Being lukewarm for God is one of the worst things that can happen to a believer. If you are **Being lukewarm for** lukewarm, you are dead. With God **God is one of the** there is no in between. You are **worst things that can** either in it or out of it. Scripture **happen to a believer.** tells us there is no middle ground. You can never balance yourself in the middle. You have a choice. Be radical for God. Don't settle for being lukewarm, which means to be fearful and afraid.

In God's eyes, it is normal and natural for us to be bold enough to brazenly talk about Jesus and violently take souls for the Kingdom of God. It is the only way to get people's attention and respect. People want to see someone who is standing firm for Jesus Christ, not someone who is always apologizing about what they preach. They retreat from the one who is so careful he can't offend important congregants in the church.

When you preach, preach what God gives you. Do not be concerned about what anybody thinks. That is what is killing the Church today. Keep God as your highest priority and finish the work He has given you today. Refuse to compromise. Refuse to surrender to the enemy. We need to change our ungodly (or godless) priorities, using Israel as an example. Starting out to rebuild the temple of God, they fell prey to opposition and lost their courage and conviction. Allowing themselves to get caught up in the attacks of the enemy, Israel let her once-focused priority to shift. It brought a rift between her and God. Hence, His blessings were withheld from her. Haggai's mission was to remedy this. His message was that God must be first. Abandoning the project altogether, they had nestled down to their personal lives and ceased building. Haggai had but one simple message to rekindle the people's zeal for building. The message was this, **Thus speaketh the Lord of hosts, saying, "This people say, The time is not come, the time that the Lord's house should be built** (Haggai 1:2). It was to encourage them to return to the Lord's command they had forsaken. What was really happening was that they had stopped building the temple of God while saying "Some day, we are going to build the house of God."

A similar mentality has taken hold in the Church. Some of you have gotten tremendous visions for the Kingdom of God, but I'm afraid you might go to the grave with those visions because you have gotten **The message of the** the "some day" doctrine. Some day **Bible is *now*.** God will give me a breakthrough. Some day God will make me a more faithful Christian. Some day I'm going to be a great prayer warrior. Some day I'm going to give God a large amount of money. On and on it goes — some day, some day, some day. The message of the Bible, however, is *now*. Now is the time for salvation. Now is the acceptable time. Not tomorrow — now. If we are going to win our nations for God, we need to bring the "Now Message" back to the Church. Only when we feel the intensity of the truth of the Now Message will Zambia and the world be saved. Hallelujah! Let your fire start to burn. Don't say some day. That is what Israel was saying. "Some day we will build the temple of God." Well, I say, as a prophet of God, that some day is now! Now is the time to win Zambia for Jesus Christ. This generation belongs to us. You and I are going to change this generation for Jesus Christ. Now is the time to do it. Live as if you could die today. This is the last hour. Look at what the book of John says regarding the Now Message.

John wrote these words almost 1,900 years ago, **"Little children...it is the last time** (1 John 2:18). One thousand nine hundred years ago, he called it the last hour. How much of the last hour has now passed? A friend of mine says this, "It is the last minute of the last second of the last hour." The hour of God is not calculated by the sun rising and setting. The Bible says that a day with the Lord is like a thousand years. Many Bible scholars don't believe we will go much beyond the year 2,000 before Jesus returns. I am not going to give any dates, but those of you caught up in material things, God is saying to you, "Change your priorities."

When God becomes your priority, then He makes yours first. God wants to bless you, your marriage, your job, whatever you touch, but you are **In this last hour, let** the problem. You have not made **us get serious with** Him a priority. In this last hour, let **our God.** us get serious with our God. Say, "I live for nobody else but God." Then, and only then will your priorities be settled. Then, you will move into the great things God has in store for you.

Once the Church changes its attitude toward God, its evangelism efforts will be strong. People will hear us and His truth through us. The Word going forth from our lips will he stronger than ever. Mighty outpourings from heaven will recompense our integrity and fill the earth with the glory of God.

## A Final World on Priorities

To be sure, God is to be our first and highest priority. Nonetheless, a word on the place of family and family provisions runs an immediate second to this supreme priority. I learned about it the hard way, but it has stuck with me ever since I got hold of the truth of it. It has to do with my being so consumed with the work of the Lord and the needs of His ministry, I overlooked the needs of my family and my own household. Not an uncommon thing, but certainly an unpleasant one. Here is what happened.

I had spent a great deal of my life in ministry. Up to last year, I was just working for the ministry. Raising money, traveling all over the world to raise money to buy the Bible college was an all-consuming activity. Through a series of blessings, we were able to purchase a sixty-two acre property to house all our operations for $130,000 which God allowed us to raise. Not long after, the Lord helped us buy vehicles for the ministry's evangelism work. Through it all, though, I had nothing for myself. My family and I were really beginning to feel the pinch of all the sacrifices, particularly when it seemed the ministry consumed all the finances and possessions that came our way.

One day my wife sat me down and said, "Honey, you travel all over the world and do a lot, but we are getting poorer and poorer. What's going on?" You know, sometimes you sow and when harvest time comes, you look as if you, yourself, are a poor man, but you are not really poor. If you have sown in faith, you have got something growing underground that is germinating. Soon it will bear fruit. As long as you give to God what He asks, you are fixed. Be confident that God is going to pay you back far above what you give to Him. Without a doubt, I knew all this and it was all turning about in my head. Still, I had to deal with the concerns of my wife that were valid.

My wife continued. "Nevers," she told me, "here is our biography. Number one, you have done much to lift up that ministry and to build that work, but we have moved from house to house, fourteen times since 1984. We have never had anything to our name. All the vehicles are bought in the name of the ministry," she concluded. I realized if I had died a year ago, my family would have had nothing. My wife reminded me that the Bible says, **A good man leaveth an inheritance to his children's children** (Proverbs 13:22). I had said, "Yeah, I am going to leave an inheritance of faith for my children."

Have you heard yourself or other pastors talk like that? Believe it, that is not what the Bible means — don't be spooked. The Bible is talking about you leaving something for your children's children. It is talking about a planned program for a definite inheritance. Many people think God does not plan, but they are wrong. God is the God of plans and planning.

God expects us to be responsible. I started to pray for God not to give me money, but wisdom. That is what Solomon prayed for. He knew, as **Providing for your** I know, that as long as he had the **family is also** wisdom of God, he had it all and **integrity.** so do I. From that incident, I learned that providing for your family, present and future, is also integrity. I determined to leave my family a fruitful inheritance.

Integrity, like every virtue of God, is productive. It brings forth fruit. Integrity's yield is called a reward. Before getting a reward, however, there is a race to be run. It must be run by the rules, and you must finish the course. My wife, Florence, and I have been running a pressing race. Many times when I felt like giving up, my wife would say, "You can't give up now, keep running." Both the heavenly and the earthly crowds are watching.

People do not respect a minister who is succeeding on the basis of charisma alone. They want to know something about his lifestyle, that there is something of substance to him as a person, that his life reflects that of Jesus Christ's. That is not always the case with most of black Africa. Their integrity suffers along with their respect from others because they think that they can somehow divorce their personal lives from their ministries. Recklessly, they live their private lives any way they want without regard to the negative effects their testimony will have on their ministry labors. They will have to take concrete steps to make integrity their priority and to let it season their fire for service in the Kingdom of God.

# The Nevers Mumba Story

I was told in my early years of ministry by my family that the choice of being a preacher was the road to poverty. I chose to obey God and made God's call a priority. My concern was the Kingdom of God. I resigned my secular employment in 1981. Doing so left me with nothing to my name: no home, no account, no family support, only a desire to serve God. Before long, I had no place to live. Being homeless, I stayed with one of my friends who had a tiny one-bedroom flat. Although I had nothing, it was the most fulfilling time of my life. I preached freely in schools, hospitals, youth camps, in markets and on street corners. Mostly, though, it was without any money being raised for an offering. Sometimes I went for as long as three months without any money, but then my host would give me an equivalent of $5.00 in U.S. currency a month when he could afford it.

In our early meetings, we have had entire schools respond to the call of salvation and demons were cast out in great numbers. It was then that Reinhard Bonnke visited our country, and through a series of events, I was asked to be the interpreter for his crusades. It was the beginning for my ministry. After interpreting for him in a few services, a special bond was created between us by the Holy Spirit.

Until Reinhard came to Zambia, I had never been exposed to power evangelism. I had only seen it in visions. Working with him I saw as many as ten thousand people jam the Gospel Tent each night. I cannot begin to describe the joy and fulfillment I felt at seeing thousands come to Christ nightly. Many received the baptism of the Holy Ghost in a miraculous way. It seemed as if a great hand held the seeking crowd and literally baptized them into the Holy Ghost. When they received, they would fall backward and start to speak with other tongues. I had never seen anything like it before.

After the crusade, Reinhard asked me about my vision in life. I explained I had been accepted to attend a Bible college in the West Indies. He looked at me and said, "Brother Nevers, I know nothing about that college, but I know something about Christ for the Nations in Dallas, Texas. It is a school that will compliment your ministry and not take away." He personally obtained the application form, and sent a letter of recommendation to Mrs. Gordon Lindsay. To my amazement, Pastor Bonnke had even taken care of my term fees.

My time in Bible college was characterized by one miracle after another. My spirit man was being prepared for the assignment of taking on a nation for God. After two years of Bible school, I returned to my home country with a vision of discipling my nation. I still had nothing to my name and spent weeks in prayer and fasting.

During this time, my would-be wife, Florence, was still in Dallas completing her year of Bible college. She returned in January 1985 and we were married April 13 of the same year. Within a year we had our first baby, but no home. By the time we had our second child, we had moved fourteen times. We kept preaching and teaching in the Bible school and, at the same time, established local churches. We kept our integrity. My desire to please God consumed me.

My experience with God has been that as I walked in integrity and in the fear of His name, He prospered me. Every car we ever owned was given to us by those who kept observing our lives.

In late 1992, God blessed us with a home. With five young children, my prayers were becoming more intense. We needed a breakthrough, but how could I afford a house? In October 1992 the answer came. I received a telephone call from a widow who had supported our ministry for years. She had lost her husband and had come to know Jesus Christ. She lived by herself and usually told me that I was her only "blood" brother, although she was white and I was black. We motivated each other and prayed for one another many times. I have not met a more sincere widow who is totally dedicated to God.

Every time I visited her I would come out with spiritual insight and revelation. For three years straight, she opened her home for my annual prayer and fasting camps. So when she called me on the phone one day and asked me to rush to her home, I did. Quickly, upon my arrival she sat me down and pulled out the Bible as usual. This time, however, there was an urgency to her actions. The woman looked at me and said, "Nevers, God spoke to me seven months ago that the house you are sitting in is your house." I almost fell off the chair. I knew I could not accept it because it was all she had. Then she took me to the scriptures, and shared how God started to speak to her and why she would not resist Him. I said, "But you are only a widow, you will need this house." She answered, "Nevers, don't stand in my way and belittle what God is doing in my life." I relented and graciously received the answer to my prayer God was providing.

I had always known God would bless us with a house, but I never thought it would be of such magnitude. Then the widow went through her moving story of how blessed she became when she decided to obey God.

The Bible says, **Neither are your ways my ways.** (Isaiah 55:8). That day I richly grasped the meaning of those words. A year later, we moved into the miracle house. As we took care of God's business, God took care of ours. He has faithfully dealt with us in this manner in every area of our lives. The miracles are too numerous to tell, but INTEGRITY has been our life and we have reaped its rewards. Walk right and God will bless you well, for the Bible says, **No good thing will he withhold from them that walk uprightly** (Psalm 84:11). Isaiah further prophesies on this subject, **He**

**that walketh righteously, and speaketh uprightly; he that despiseth the gain of oppressions, that shaketh his hands from holding of bribes, that stoppeth his ears from hearing of blood, and shutteth his eyes from seeing evil; he shall dwell on high: his place of defense shall be the munitions of rocks: bread shall be given him; his waters shall be sure.** (Isaiah 33:15,16).

Right priorities will enhance your integrity!

# Commitment to a Life of Integrity

Search my heart, O God, and see if there by any wicked way in me. I know that Your plans are good for me according to Jeremiah 29:11, but You desire that my ways please You. Forgive me for walking in compromise, lies and deceit. I repent, Lord Jesus. May I be an instrument of praise in Your hands. Forgive me for jealousy, envy, pride and a lack of fear of You.

I now commit myself to a walk of holiness and integrity. I pray for my family, church and nation. Use me to influence my generation through integrity of heart. I love You, Lord, and thank You for answering my prayer. To God be the Glory! In Jesus' name, Amen.

**You can obtain additional materials by
Evangelist Nevers Mumba from:**

Victory Ministries, Inc.
P. O. Box 22656
Kitwe, Zambia, AFRICA


**Latest Releases:**

1. Steps to the Supernatural
2. Taking Hold of the Nations
3. Getting Back to the Basics
4. Strategy for Revival


Subscribe to Nevers Mumba's
quarterly newspaper,
*The Victory Report*